A History of

MYSTIC

Connecticut

D1225354

A History of

MYSTIC

CONNECTICUT

FROM PEQUOT VILLAGE TO TOURIST TOWN

LEIGH FOUGHT

THE
History
PRESS

Published by The History Press
Charleston, SC 29403
www.historypress.net

Cover image: Morgan and Conrad. Photo by Stephen Sisk (www.stephensiskphotography.com). Courtesy of Mystic Seaport, Mystic, Connecticut (www.mysticseaport.org).

First published 2007
Second printing 2013

Manufactured in the United States

ISBN 978.1.59629.221.5

Library of Congress CIP data applied for.

For Huw,
All you need…

CONTENTS

Acknowledgements   9

Tour of the Town: An Introduction to Mystic's History   11

Chapter 1   The Pequot Village, the Mystic River to 1638   13

Chapter 2   Emerging English Settlement, 1645–1700   31

Chapter 3   The Villages and the Atlantic World, 1700–1815   44

Chapter 4   A Village of Shipyards, 1815–1914   59

Chapter 5   A Village of Factories, 1815–1940   78

Chapter 6   A Resort Community in a Progressive Age, 1870–1940   87

Chapter 7   Tourist Town, 1940–2001   121

Researching Mystic   141

Selected Bibliography   143

Index   147

About the Author   157

ACKNOWLEDGEMENTS

In 2001, as a Mystic Seaport intern, I searched in vain for a comprehensive survey of Mystic's history. This is the result of my search for that book. Thank you to everyone at The History Press for publishing this work. Thank you to those other interns from that summer—Julia, Davison, Jill, Jessica, Kristi, Kirsti, Alyssa and the two Jeffs—the first people to think that such a book would be worth reading.

This book would not have been possible without the help of the archivists and librarians at all of the local repositories across Groton and Stonington, including Rodi York, Kathleen Foulke and Amy German in the Research and Collections Department at Mystic Seaport; Anne Tate at the Richard W. Woolworth Library of Stonington Historical Society; Betty Noyse at the Mystic River Historical Society; and especially Michael A. Spellmon at both the Indian and Colonial Research Center and the Groton Public Library. Also at Mystic Seaport, thanks go to Andy Price, Bernie Kalinowski and Steve Sisk. Thank you to Professor John Y. Simon, Aaron Lisec and Dawn Vogel at the U.S. Grant Association for their patience in allowing me to complete this volume. On the homefront, I am always grateful for the entire corps of Foughts, who include Louis, Glenna, Karl, Laurie, Jake, Keith, Sharon and Bradley and Catherine McKenzie, and for Babu Srinivasan, Dwight Watson, Melissa Bingman and, of course, Huw Powell, who would never keep me apart from the things that I love.

AN INTRODUCTION TO MYSTIC'S HISTORY

Mystic has a lot of history," say tourists, transplants and natives; and each year, thousands of visitors flock to see this history and to enjoy such local attractions as Mystic Seaport, the Mystic Marinelife Aquarium, the surrounding coast and the nearby Mashantucket Pequot Museum & Research Center. Yet there is a constant demand to know, as many ask, "What was it like here *then?*" The question is well asked because the quaint downtown and poetic name belie a grittier past of warfare and privateering, shipbuilding and manufacturing. Indeed, much of Mystic as it appears today, including the name "Mystic," is a product of developments in only the past century.

Many volumes have chronicled various aspects of Mystic's past, but this particular volume surveys Mystic's history from the time of Pequot habitation in the early seventeenth century to the year 2001. The narrative will revolve around the village of Mystic on the eastern and western banks of the Mystic River, as well as the village of Old Mystic at the head of the river. Sources and events in the course of Mystic's history, however, may force the scope of the narrative periodically to encompass population centers surrounding Mystic.

Additionally, five overlapping phases of Mystic's history will emerge in this narrative. The first follows the rise and fall of the Pequot nation in southeastern Connecticut, culminating with the English attack on their homes on the Mystic River. The second traces English colonization of Mystic and its growth as a village of subsistence and smuggling through the American Revolution and War of 1812. The third phase encompasses Mystic's golden age as a center of shipbuilding and overlaps the fourth phase of manufacturing. The final phase describes Mystic's development into a vacation destination, beginning with the "summer people" of the late nineteenth century and growing with the post–World War II rise of "heritage tourism." This volume ends in the year 2001 because the effects of September 11, rising gas prices and altering trends in tourism on the local economy are not yet distinguishable as temporary crises or part of ongoing trends that signal a new phase in Mystic's history.

CHAPTER 1

THE PEQUOT VILLAGE, THE MYSTIC RIVER TO 1638

The Pequot built the first known village on the river on the crest of a hill overlooking the western bank of the Mystic River, then called the Siccanemos. The only written records of this village describe it as having existed in 1637, surrounded by a palisade of tree trunks and inhabited primarily by women, children and the elderly. The able-bodied men congregated at the more exposed Fort Hill village six miles to the southwest or traveled among various villages as necessity dictated. Additionally, records of other Native American villages in the region, including larger and more strategically located villages on the Thames River, do not describe encircling walls or any other sort of man-made protection. This was the first for the Pequot. The Pequot nation had reached a crucial point in its history by 1637, and the Siccanemos village may have been fortified in anticipation of an armed conflict.

For several decades prior to 1637, the Pequot had been building an empire across eastern Connecticut. Historians for many years believed that this development was an outgrowth of their migration from eastern New York in the late sixteenth century. Archaeological evidence now suggests that the Pequot were actually indigenous to southeastern Connecticut, a conceivable theory since evidence also exists of very ancient people who lived in a region called Gungywump, slightly northwest of the Mystic River. In 1614, Dutch mapmaker Adrien Block, in the first written record of the Pequot, showed them occupying the land between the rivers later called Niantic and Thames. By 1637, when the village on the Mystic became important, the Pequot had gained control of a wide territory extending toward the Pawcatuck River on the east and the Connecticut River on the west. This territory included not only navigable waterways deep into the interior, but the coast as well. Most of the Pequot expansion took place during the 1620s and 1630s, when Europeans became a factor in Native American intertribal relations.

Despite an initial hostile encounter with Dutch traders in 1622, the Pequot entered into an ongoing exchange with them for the two most important commodities passing between Europeans and Native Americans: furs and wampum. Wampum may

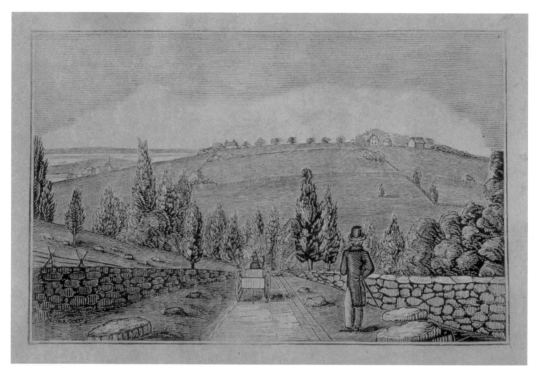

In 1836, John Warner Barber drew this image of Pequot Hill, the site of the Pequot Mystic village two centuries earlier. Typical of European-style farming, the hill itself had been deforested during the intervening centuries. *John Warner Barber Collection, Graphics Collection, Connecticut Historical Society.*

have been the more important of these, serving as currency from the Atlantic coast northward into the Iroquois Five Nations. By controlling parts of the coast, the Pequot had access to the whelk shells and quahog that provided the raw materials for making the purple and white beads of wampum strings and belts. Their position along the rivers allowed them to control trade of all commodities deeper into the continent, acting as the powerful middlemen between the weaker tribes to the north and the Europeans to the east. The initial threat from the Dutch traders, however, may have kept the Pequot on their guard against the Europeans.

Beginning with this base of trade on the coast, the Pequot began to expand their influence. They defeated the sachem of a smaller tribe along the Connecticut River, and formed alliances with the other tribes in that vicinity that favored the Pequot, while reducing the Connecticut River tribes to vassals. The Pequot repeated this pattern throughout southeastern Connecticut, extending their influence to the mouth of the Connecticut River, the eastern end of Long Island, Block Island and the small, tidal river called Sassacus. There, they crept dangerously close to territory claimed by the Narragansett.

By 1637, the Pequot controlled some of the most strategic territory in their part of the continent. To the northwest, after a series of wars, the Five Nations of the Iroquois dominated the land between the Hudson River and the Great Lakes and extended their influence east into central New England. All trade between the Dutch at the mouth of the Hudson River and the French on the St. Lawrence to the north flowed through the Iroquois. The Pequot, however, lay just far enough outside of this sphere of influence to be safe from any threat the Iroquois presented. The Pequot's control of the lower Connecticut River provided them access to the eastern allies of the Iroquois farther north on the river, who seized the opportunity to become a source of Pequot wampum for the Five Nations.

To the east of the Pequot lay the Narragansett, who presented a closer potential challenge to the growing Pequot empire. The Narragansett held a comparable position in relation to the tribes to their east as the Pequot did to the tribes to their north and west. The Native American tribes who lived on the coast from Cape Cod to Nova Scotia had been the first indigenous people to come into contact with Europeans. That meant that they were also the first to experience the full force of European diseases. Smallpox, bubonic plague, measles and a whole host of other illnesses ran rampant, depopulating whole villages at a time and killing between 55 and 95 percent of the coastal people. The Narragansett had evaded some of this scourge because they lived at a distance from the initial point of contact with the Europeans for long enough of a time to develop some resistance to the European diseases. The Narragansett Bay also provided a barrier between their population and the English who were settling Plymouth. Their relative strength and greater numbers allowed them to provide asylum and a native ally to the eastern tribes. Their strength grew when they established trade ties to both the English at Massachusetts Bay and the Dutch at Manhattan. Until the Pequot moved east of the Mystic River, the two tribes avoided direct conflict.

As for European nations, the Pequot lay at an advantageous point between the Dutch and the English. To the east of the Pequot, the English had begun to gain a toehold on the continent along Massachusetts Bay during the 1620s. Separatists from the Church of England and the "outsiders" who accompanied them on the *Mayflower* settled Plymouth Plantation in 1620. They found themselves reliant on the Native American population for survival, although relations between the two cultures remained tenuous, if not overtly hostile, for many decades. The uneasy alliance, however, allowed the Plymouth colonists to establish trade relations as far west as Narragansett Bay, if not with the Narragansett nation itself. Soon after, the English settlers also began to trade with the Dutch.

At the same time as settlement of the Plymouth Colony, the Massachusetts Bay Company had begun making inroads from Cape Ann down to the Shawmut peninsula (Boston). The company succeeded in establishing trade ties with the Native American tribes, extending northward up the Maine coast. As with Plymouth, the Massachusetts Bay colonists were both dependant upon and hostile toward the native population. Moreover, both colonies had a rather unsophisticated understanding of the politics in and among the various native tribes.

Each of these English colonies was a company in competition with all other colonies for revenue produced by the fur and wampum trade. Often, the only factor that united these separate entities was their allegiance to the English government. Thus, the Massachusetts Bay and Plymouth Colonies did not necessarily cooperate with

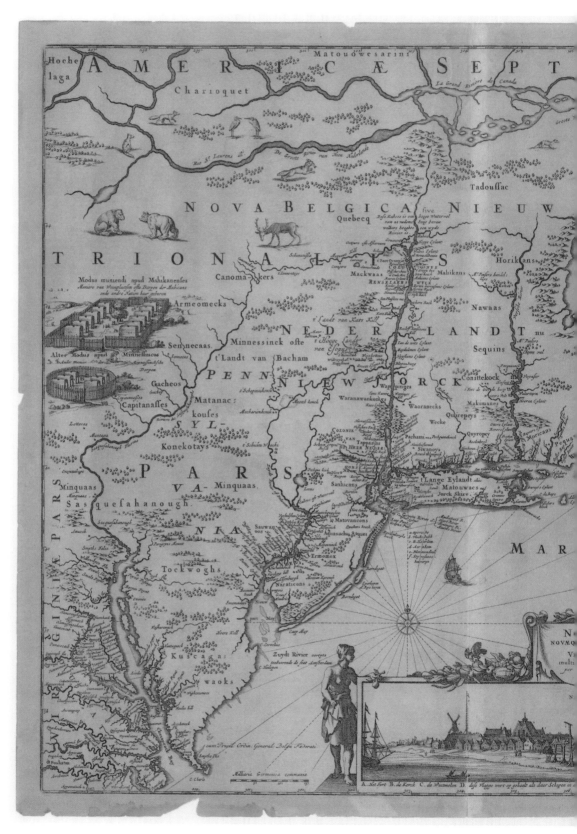

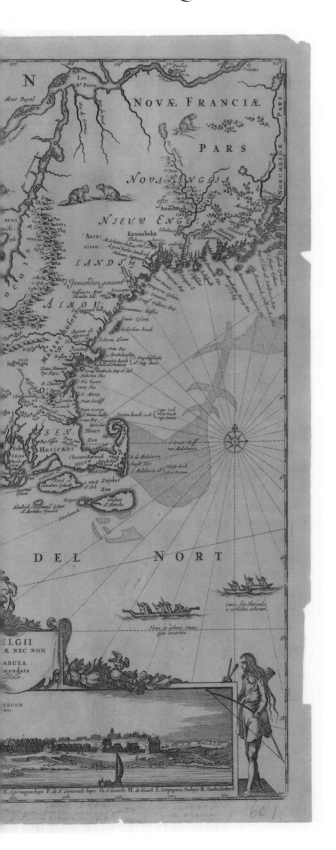

"Novi Belgii Novaeque Angliae nec non parties Virginiae tabulat multis in Locis emendata per Nicolaum Visscher," a 1685 map showing the location of various native tribes. The Pequot territory, labeled "Pequotoos," lies along the Thames River between the "Wampanoos" and the Mohican. *Mystic Seaport Collection, Mystic, Connecticut, G3715 1685.V5.*

one another, and each formed alliances with different, sometimes competing Native American nations.

The Pequot lay outside of immediate contact with these English colonies, but trusted neither. They perhaps also viewed, or pretended to view, the relationship between the two groups of English settlers with the same lack of sophisticated understanding that English settlers viewed the relationship among Native Americans. The Pequot, however, did fully comprehend the uses of all of these relationships—English to English and English to Native American—in their quest to expand and consolidate their control of resources in the region.

The Dutch also presented opportunities to exploit the competing relationships surrounding the Pequot's territory. To the west, the Dutch had established an outpost on the southern tip of Manhattan Island. From there, they extended their influence up the Hudson River to the Five Nations. To the east, they had established trade ties with Native American nations as far along the coast as Narragansett Bay. Beyond lay the Plymouth Colony that, while English, had some familiarity with the Netherlands. They also had access to wampum beads and furs from the Maine coast, which would present competition with the Pequot beads and furs, thereby placing the Dutch and the Plymouth colonists in a favorable bargaining position for prices, both in relation to one another and, more importantly, in relation to the Native American tribes with whom they traded. Thus, the Dutch began trade with Plymouth in 1627, five years after they had begun trading with the Pequot.

Between Manhattan and Narragansett Bay, the Dutch had identified the Connecticut River as one of the few navigable rivers that led deep into the interior of the continent. In 1632, they sailed upriver to establish the post Good Hope at the confluence of the Connecticut and Little Rivers, near the site that (in a few years) would become Hartford. The Pequot, from whom the Dutch purchased the land, insisted upon a monopoly on trade for themselves and their allied tribes at the post. After nearly a year of hostilities, the Pequot agreed to allow other tribes to trade at Good Hope. This reluctant concession may or may not have had a direct bearing on subsequent events, but the establishment of this Dutch trading post certainly set in motion actions that would lead the entire region between the Connecticut River and Massachusetts Bay to war within five years.

Until 1632, the Pequot had been able to exploit their distance from the Dutch, the English, the Narragansett and the Iroquois due to their location and their ability to subjugate smaller, less powerful tribes. When the Dutch established Good Hope and refused the Pequot a monopoly at the post, they introduced outsiders into that territory whom the Pequot could not control. This began an erosion of Pequot influence as competitors maneuvered to expand their own influence into the Pequot land and weaken the Pequot's hold on fur and wampum sources.

The group of Connecticut River tribes became the first to seize upon the opportunity to chip away at Pequot control. As the Pequot and Dutch negotiated over the terms of Good Hope, representatives of these river tribes traveled to Massachusetts Bay to invite the Puritans to establish their own post in the same area. An English outpost on the Connecticut River, one in closer alignment with these tribes, might counterbalance the Dutch and their Pequot, Narragansett and Iroquois allies. The English, meanwhile, could use the Connecticut River to expand farther into the country, surrounding all the tribes of southern New England and opening diplomatic relations with the Iroquois. By 1634, the two English trading posts of Windsor and Wethersfield had sprung up on the river. They were followed by the settlement of Hartford in 1636. Due to their distance from Massachusetts Bay, however, these settlements operated with relative independence from the main colony, establishing their own government or court to oversee their management.

Meanwhile, before these sites could be settled, the use of the land had to be negotiated with the Native American occupants. The Massachusetts Bay colonists conducted these negotiations with the Connecticut River tribes, without the approval of the Pequot. As a result, the Pequot considered the English along the river to be interlopers and eyed them with suspicion and hostility.

In 1634, just as the Massachusetts Bay post made its appearance, the Pequot and the Dutch proved that they had not entirely resolved their differences over Good Hope. The Pequot and Narragansett had increased hostilities toward one another when the post appeared. The Narragansett passed through or near Pequot territory on their way to the Dutch post, and the Pequot resented the Narragansett's ability to encroach upon their territory to the point that a Pequot band attacked and killed a Narragansett band on its way to trade at Good Hope. Whether or not this band was in fact Narragansett remains in dispute. They were, however, de facto allies of the Dutch by virtue of their desire to trade at the Dutch post. By attacking them en route to the post, the Pequot had violated their agreement to allow all other parties to trade there. In retaliation for this violation, the Dutch captured the highest sachem or leader of the Pequot, Tatobem, and demanded ransom in wampum; although the ransom was paid, the Dutch executed Tatobem.

The murder of Tatobem sparked two conflicts in the Pequot nation. The first was an escalation of hostilities toward Massachusetts Bay. The second was a power struggle among the heirs to Tatobem's position. Both undercut the Pequot's strength with disastrous results.

According to the Pequot' tradition, and in fact the tradition of most other native nations of the eastern North American seaboard, a price must be exacted for a murder. This could be a payment of wampum to the deceased's family or retribution, one life for another. The Pequot sought retribution, which led to the death of John Stone in early 1634.

Stone was an English "adventurer," one of many free agents trading up and down the North American coast from Massachusetts to the West Indies. He had traded in Massachusetts Bay, but was asked to leave the colony for his less-than-Puritanical ways. On his way back south, he was attacked and killed near the mouth of the Connecticut River. According to one story, while trading on shore, he had kidnapped a group of Pequot in order to sell them into slavery, and he was killed by their rescue party. According to another, the Pequot had used trade as a ruse to gain access to Stone's ship in order to assassinate him.

Infuriated, the leadership at Massachusetts Bay interpreted the death of Stone as a declaration of war. In October 1634, a delegation of Pequot traveled to Massachusetts

Bay to assure the colonists that they in no way intended to go to war against the English. They took full responsibility for the death of Stone, and offered Governor Roger Ludlow payment for Stone's death. They also insisted that they had mistaken Stone's ship for a Dutch ship and had attacked it under that assumption and in retribution for the death of Tatobem.

The Massachusetts Bay colonists, however, rejected this explanation. They argued that the Pequot must surely have recognized the difference between a Dutch and an English ship. Furthermore, the English dealt with murder differently. They refused the Pequot's payment as justice for Stone's death. Instead, in a second meeting with the Pequot a month later, the Massachusetts Bay government seized the opportunity to expand their own claims in New England. They demanded that Stone's killers be handed over to meet European justice; that a ransom in wampum worth 250 pounds sterling be paid; that the Pequot cede all of their land to the Massachusetts Bay Colony; that the Pequot trade only with the English; and that all disputes between the Pequot and the Narragansett be mediated by the English. This enormous concession of autonomy far exceeded anything that the Pequot anticipated. The Pequot delegation, however, seemed to agree to the settlement and returned home, but Tatobem's successor, Sassacus, rejected and thereby nullified the agreement.

Sassacus's rise to power in the wake of Tatobem's murder had destabilized internal Pequot politics. While the Pequot leadership was dispersed among the various villages, each with a sachem, all villages deferred to one central sachem. This had been Tatobem's position. With his death, two factions formed around two lower sachems claiming Tatobem's position: Tatobem's son, Sassacus, and Tatobem's son-in-law, Uncas. When Sassacus emerged victorious from this competition, Uncas defected from the Pequot nation.

Uncas was sachem of the villages around the Niantic River, whose residents called themselves Mohegan. He had already caused problems for the Pequot leaders prior to 1634, having been briefly exiled before Tatobem's death. His subsequent behavior indicates that he probably believed an alliance with the Narragansett to be prudent as Europeans moved ever closer to the Pequot and Narragansett territory. Uncas certainly had a very friendly relationship with the Narragansett. They had accepted him in his exile prior to his challenge of Sassacus's leadership. When he defected after Sassacus's election, he brought with him his Mohegan villages. Shortly thereafter, Uncas returned to the Pequot fold, begging forgiveness and swearing allegiance to Sassacus. Nevertheless, he soon returned to the Narragansett. Shortly thereafter, he again returned to Sassacus, swearing allegiance and begging forgiveness, which Sassacus granted. This cycle occurred five times over the next three years.

Two other tributary sachems, Wequash and Sosos, had also left the Pequot nation to join the Narragansett. Sosos was sachem of the Niantic villages on the eastern reaches of Pequot territory at the Pawcatuck River, and his people had been one of the Pequot's closest allies. Sosos, however, severed his ties to the Pequot in 1636 when he betrayed the Pequot war party with which he was traveling and killed its leader.

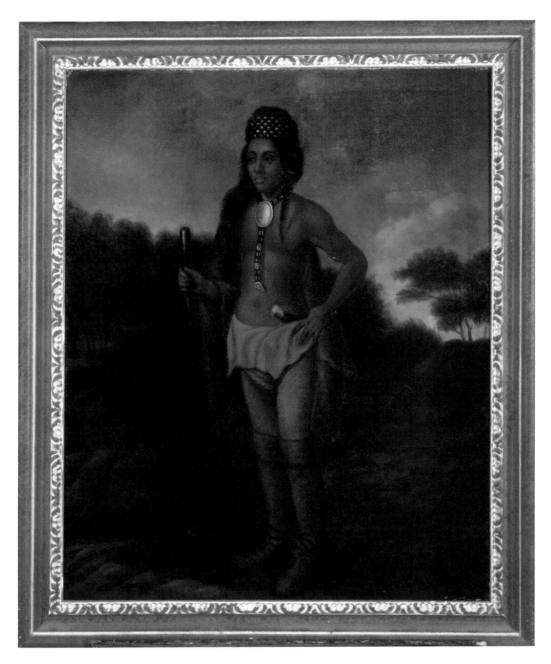

This nineteenth-century painting by Charles Osgood was originally believed to be of the Narragansett sachem Ninigret. Art history scholars at Brown University now believe it to be of a Pequot sachem. *Massachusetts Historical Society.*

Sassacus then found himself in a precarious position within his own nation. His villages lay in the vicinity of the Siccanemos River, one overlooking the river and the other overlooking the mouth of the river to the east, Long Island Sound to the south and the Poquonnoc plains to the west. He also retained the loyalty of villages along the Thames River, which was called the Pequot River by the English. Yet surrounding these villages were those of Uncas. Moreover, the rebelling sachem had the support of the Narragansett, and the Narragansett had the support of the Iroquois far up along the Hudson River, the Connecticut River tribes and the English at Massachusetts Bay. In fact, any faction with any grudge against the Pequot gradually aligned itself with these Pequot enemies. The Dutch, too, kept their distance. Sassacus and his people were dangerously alienated from all surrounding nations, with no allies for assistance.

In 1636, hostilities escalated into an undeclared war. In March, engineer Lion Gardiner established Fort Saybrook to protect the mouth of the Connecticut River for Massachusetts Bay traders. Gardiner understood the delicacies and dangers of diplomacy this far from European centers, and repeatedly counseled caution. He believed that the Massachusetts Bay government should not continue its demands for harsh retribution in the matter of John Stone's death because the Pequot retaliation would disrupt trade and place the Massachusetts Bay settlements, including Fort Saybrook, in grave danger. Gardiner could not afford to defend the fort or the Connecticut River settlements until the fort was able to feed and shelter itself.

Among the fifty men who joined Gardiner there were Thomas Stanton (circa 1608–1677) and John Oldham. The twenty-year-old Stanton was one of the few Englishmen who knew the Algonquin language spoken by all Native American tribes in the area, including the Pequot. He had emigrated from England to Virginia only two years earlier, living for some time among the Indians there before migrating to Massachusetts Bay in 1635. His linguistic skill made him a valuable asset to the colony's trade and diplomacy, thereby providing him a means of making his own fortune. For just such reasons he went to Connecticut as one of the early founders of Hartford. John Oldham was a trader and had been one of the founders of Wethersfield. His fate would have dire consequences for the Pequot.

In July, Oldham sailed to Block Island to trade. There, a group of Native Americans boarded his vessel, killed Oldham and his crew and took control of the ship and its cargo. A passing vessel commanded by John Gallup noticed something odd about the set of the sails on Oldham's ship and cruised closer to investigate. Seeing no Englishmen on deck, Gallup fired upon the vessel, shocking the Native Americans aboard. In the ensuing battle, most of the Native Americans either escaped or were killed, with the exception of two prisoners. Since the Block Island tribes were known allies of the Pequot, the Pequot received the blame for the attack. The Narragansett later claimed responsibility, offering to pay tribute and apprehend those responsible for Oldham and his crew's deaths, according to English demands. They also solidified a limited but formal alliance with Massachusetts Bay, agreeing not to support the Pequot against the colony should open hostilities break out. Despite the actions of the Narragansett, the Massachusetts Bay colonists continued to blame the Pequot for the attack on Oldham's ship, sending a military expedition under Captain John Endicott to retrieve the killers of both Oldham and Stone.

Endicott, along with Captains John Underhill and William Turner and a force of ninety men, sailed to Block Island. While they were allegedly there to apprehend the individuals responsible for the death of Oldham, they actually intended to attack the entire island. When they arrived, however, they found that the island tribes had evacuated. Undaunted, Endicott sailed for Fort Saybrook, intending to launch an

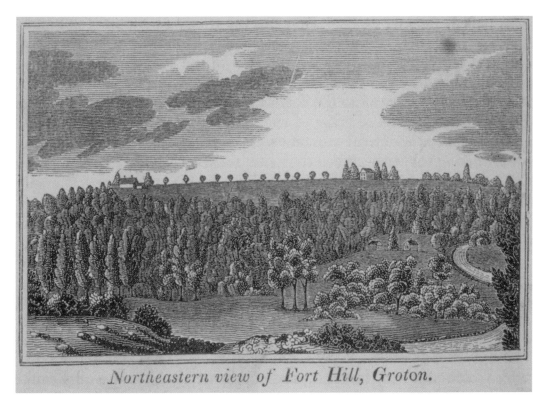

Northeastern view of Fort Hill, Groton.

An 1836 image of Fort Hill, the location of Sassacus's village, southwest of Mystic. *John Warner Barber Collection, Graphics Collection, Connecticut Historical Society.*

expedition against the Pequot from there. An unenthusiastic Gardiner met them with the accusation, "You come hither to raise these wasps about my ears, then you will take wind and flee away." Endicott dismissed Gardiner and proceeded with his plans.

The Massachusetts Bay force advanced to the Pequot (Thames) River, where a Pequot village sat on the rocky highlands on its east side. Endicott and his men approached the village, demanding that the Pequot men meet them in battle. When the Pequot expressed a preference for negotiation, Endicott ordered the village attacked and crops burned.

Gardiner's accusations proved prescient. The Pequot interpreted this wholesale attack on an entire village as a declaration of war. In the following months, they launched a counteroffensive against the English settlements on the Connecticut River. They lay siege to Fort Saybrook through the autumn and winter of 1636 and into the spring of 1637, capturing, torturing and killing anyone who ventured outside of its walls. They also made overtures to their longtime enemies, the Narragansett, attempting to persuade them into an alliance against the English. The Narragansett refused, then allied with the Massachusetts Bay colonists, an agreement that was solemnized with the gift of five severed Pequot hands.

Then, in April 1637, the Pequot attacked the settlement at Wethersfield, killing all but two young women, whom they took prisoner. The Connecticut River settlements, governing themselves from Hartford, had remained closely tied to Massachusetts Bay. Officials of that colony had attended to Native American diplomacy up to this point. The attack on Wethersfield hitting so near to the other settlements, however, became a matter of home defense. These Indian settlements did not demand the apprehension of those responsible for the attack, as the Massachusetts Bay government had done for the deaths of Stone and Oldham. They did not demand a bounty in furs or wampum, nor did they intend to attack one Pequot village as revenge for the Pequot attack on one English village. Instead, they declared war on the entire Pequot nation, with the intention of permanently eliminating the Pequot people as a force in southern New England.

To this end, the Connecticut River settlements raised an army under Captain John Mason, a professional soldier. The thirty-seven-year-old Mason had emigrated from England in 1630 and settled in Windsor in 1635. Since few of the colonists had formal military training, he emerged as their leader. A devoutly religious Puritan, he saw his mission not only as a measure for the protection of his community, but also as a holy war. The assault on the Pequot was a test of his moral fortitude in the face of what he considered an essentially evil opponent. When he later wrote his account of the war, he did so "for the help of this thou mayest look backward and interpret how GOD hath been working, and that very wonderfully for thy Safety and Comfort. And it being the LORD's *doing*, it should be *marvelous in thine Eyes*." Captain John Underhill went further in his own justification, comparing the war on the Pequot to the Biblical account of David's war.

In May 1637, Mason launched his expedition of ninety men, including Thomas Stanton as interpreter, against the Pequot. Uncas also joined the fight, bringing along seventy of his own men. Uncas made clear that he operated in tandem with Mason, not as a subordinate, and he and his men were not mustered into the Connecticut forces, as was sometimes the practice with colonial militia. This joint force sailed down the Connecticut River from Hartford to Fort Saybrook, where Underhill's force of twenty men joined them.

From Saybrook, the forces of Mason, Underhill and Uncas sailed westward to meet the Narragansett sachem Miantonomo. Although Mason's orders directed him to land in the Pequot River and attack the villages along its banks, he did not have the firepower to launch a naval attack. That approach also carried the danger of meeting a Pequot force armed with muskets, since the Pequot had reportedly captured sixteen firearms. Instead, Mason hoped to attack the Pequot by land. Such a maneuver would carry an element of surprise by eliminating the spectacle of landing a vessel. The shortest route to the targeted Pequot villages started in the Narragansett territory and allowed a rear approach. Additionally, the Narragansett might be counted upon to protect Mason. Indeed, Miantonomo reinforced Mason's group with five hundred of his own men.

Mason, Underhill, Uncas, their forces and those of Miantonomo began their march westward from the Pawcatuck River northwest toward the head of the Mystic River. After two days, they found themselves amid cornfields. Uncas and the Narragansett assured Mason that they were nearing two Pequot villages. Mason hoped to attack both

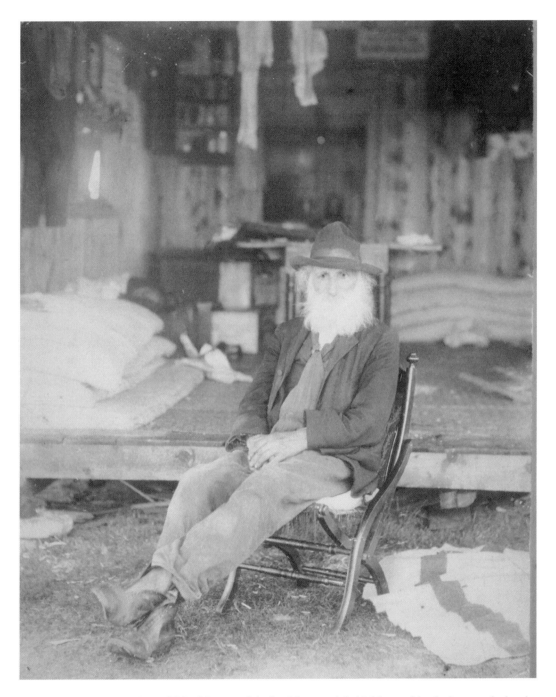

Andrew Mason, a descendant of John Mason and the last Mason to inhabit Masons Island, photographed at the end of the nineteenth century. *Mystic Seaport Collection, Mystic, Connecticut, #46.700.*

at once, but upon learning that they were too far apart to make that plan feasible, he reluctantly settled upon the nearer one and left the farther one for a later battle. "We were much grieved," he later wrote, "chiefly because the greatest and bloodiest Sachem there resided, whose name was Sassacous [*sic*]."

The company marched toward that nearer village until sunset. "Coming to a little Swamp between two Hills," recalled Mason, "there we pitched our little Camp." Underhill described the camp as lying about two miles away from the village. Tradition places this site along the western bank of the Mystic River at a rocky outcrop called Porter's Rocks. The sentries, stationed at a distance, could hear the village inhabitants singing that night.

The next morning, May 26, 1637, the forces awoke at dawn, slightly later than intended. The English gathered to pray. Then, with the Native Americans leading and following, the expedition began their approach to that palisaded village on the crest of the hill above the Mystic River. Underhill circled around to the south while Mason arrayed his men to the west. The Native Americans, now numbering around three hundred, moved behind the English. Already, the village inhabitants were rising. A dog, sensing the approach of intruders, barked. "Owanux!" a voice cried, "Owanux!" This warning translated was "Englishmen!" The attack began.

The English, encircling the village, fired a volley over the walls. A wail arose from within. The English approached the two entrances, but the Pequot had wedged branches into the openings. Mason climbed over the barrier. The others pulled and tugged at the obstacles. The Pequot inside the village rallied for a counterattack. John (or William) Hedge of Underhill's company was at the front and received wounds in both arms. Yet the defense was not enough to repel the English. They cleared the path and spilled into the village. There the fight continued. The Pequot continued to fire arrows at the invaders. Several blows landed upon Mason's head, and Underhill received shots to the hip and neck. While two of the colonists were killed, most of the arrows glanced off the metal helmets and breastplates of the English soldiers' uniforms. Mason and Underhill emerged with only slight wounds.

Mason decided that the destruction of the village in hand-to-hand combat would take too much time and energy. He emerged from a wigwam carrying a torch and, forfeiting any chance to plunder the village, set fire to the nearest structure and ordered the whole village burned. Soon, the entire west side was ablaze. Underhill ran a line of powder along the other side of the village and set it aflame. The English retreated outside of the walls. Inside, some of the Pequot continued to fight until the fire burned the strings from their bows. Others, blistered and bleeding, attempted to escape over the walls, only to meet with the English, who indiscriminately "entertained with the point of the sword." The encircling forces of Uncas and the Narragansett cut down those who slipped through the English lines. Only seven Pequot escaped, with another seven being taken prisoner. The village burned to the ground inside of an hour.

"Thus did the Lord judge among heathens, filling the Place with dead Bodies!" Mason pronounced. "Should not Christians have more mercy and compassion?" Underhill later questioned. "Sometimes the Scripture declareth women and children must perish with their parents," he concluded. "Sometimes the case alters; but we will not dispute it now. We had sufficient light from the word of God for our proceedings."

Estimates of the Pequot dead vary. Underhill reported four hundred people inside the village. Mason insisted there were as many as seven hundred. The English lost two men, with twenty others wounded. The Narragansett perhaps gave the most accurate

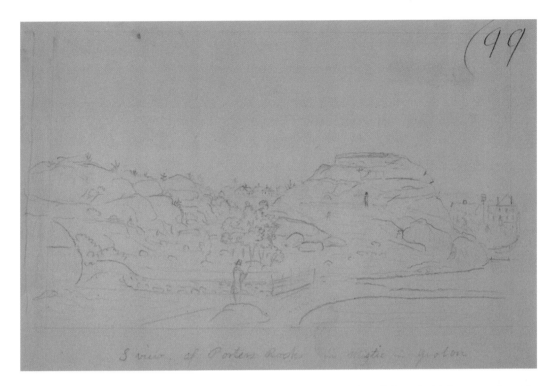

Drawn about 1836, this early image depicts Porter's Rocks, the campsite of the colonial forces on the night before their attack on the Mystic Pequot village. Porter's Rocks, heavily quarried in the late nineteenth century, lies toward the head of the Mystic River. *John Warner Barber Collection, Graphics Collection, Connecticut Historical Society.*

impression of the attack. Although they had been participants in the slaughter, they abandoned the English by the end of the day, repelled by the total war tactics that would destroy an entire population. "It is naught," they told Underhill, "because it is too furious and slays too many men." Only Uncas and his men remained.

The English forces could not relish their victory for long. With the village reduced to embers before noon, Mason realized that his men did not have enough provisions to care for their wounded. In the midst of this realization, a force of 150 to 300 Pequot attacked. This group had come from the second village at Fort Hill, six miles to the southwest. Seeing the smoke from the burning village upriver, they rushed to the rescue. Too late to save their kin, they set upon the attackers. A running skirmish ensued, each party alternately pursuing the other with the English facing defeat. Then the vessel that had taken the combined forces of Uncas and the English from Saybrook to the Narragansett territory appeared. The now ragged expedition clamored aboard and was carried to safety in the Thames River harbor.

The news of the massacre at Mystic spread quickly throughout Pequot territory. The English now hunted the Pequot, slaughtering and enslaving the Pequot people and anyone who aided them. Throughout the summer, villages evacuated, hoping to find safety on Long Island or among distant tribes. They quickly found themselves rejected by all of their former allies.

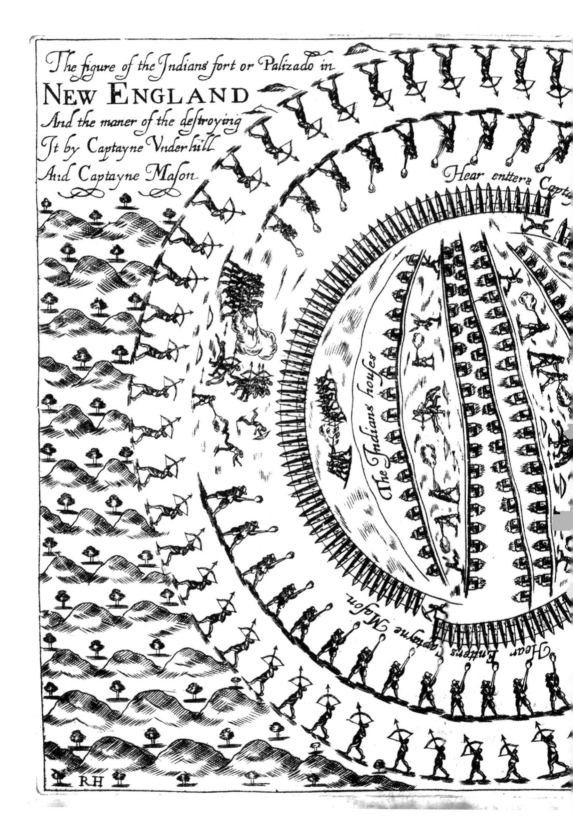

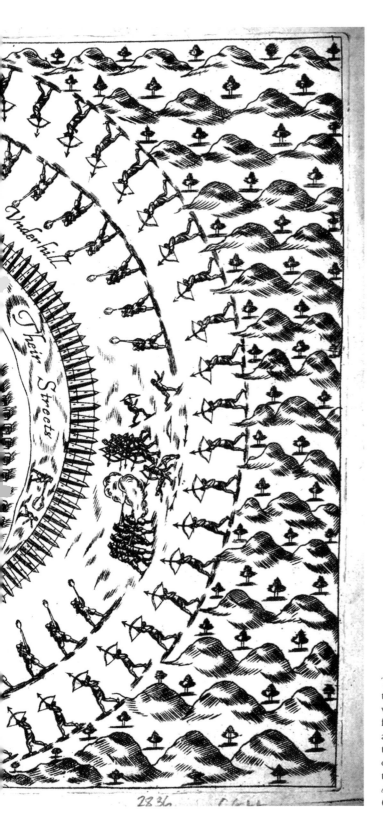

This earliest image of Mystic depicts the English attack on the Pequot village in 1637, and appeared as the frontispiece of John Underhill's 1638 account. Although highly stylized, this image suggests the arrangement of longhouses, gardens and walls of the village. *Mashantucket Pequot Museum and Research Center, Archives and Special Collections, MSS 52, Newes from America.*

Sassacus, leading four hundred men, women and children, set a course for the Five Nations. Mason and his men, however, trapped the group in a swamp near the site that would become the town of Fairfield. Thomas Stanton negotiated with Sassacus, persuading him to release the women, children and elderly to the English with the promise that they would not be killed. Sassacus agreed, and over half of the Pequot trapped in the swamp emerged. They were enslaved and distributed among various Native American tribes and European slave traders. The English then attacked the remaining men in the swamp. Sassacus escaped along with eighty men, fleeing to the Mohawk on the Hudson River. Instead of finding asylum, he and his men were killed. The Mohawk sent his head, according to some reports, or his scalp, according to others, to the Connecticut General Court at Hartford.

The English were not satisfied with the mere death of Sassacus, nor with breaking the Pequot's power. They had intended to eradicate the Pequot in ways that later centuries would term "genocide," and pursued that end with the Treaty of Hartford. This document, signed on September 21, 1638, officially ended the Pequot War. The English settlements on the Connecticut River claimed the Pequot land by "right of conquest." The surviving Pequot were handed over to the Narragansett, the Mohawk and Uncas's Mohegan. The Pequot survivors were forbidden to speak their own dialect, practice their own religion, form their own village governments or in any way claim tribal distinction as Pequot. Even the very name "Pequot" became forbidden.

The first community on the Mystic River had met with disaster. Sitting upriver, far from exposure to passing English ships and virtually unknown to Europeans before that fateful day in May 1637, it had provided protection for its several hundred inhabitants. As the Pequot nation became increasingly important, its location between the Narragansett and the Thames River villages of its own nation placed the Mystic village directly in harm's way. The destruction of this village signaled the end of Pequot domination in southeastern Connecticut and opened the land to settlement by the English.

CHAPTER 2

EMERGING ENGLISH
SETTLEMENT, 1645–1700

Contrary to expectations and later interpretations, the end of the Pequot War in 1638 did not bring an immediate rush of settlers to the Mystic River, which was not considered of particular importance in these colonial years. As an estuary, the Mystic did not provide the essential needs that the colonists required of a river. The water flowed in and out with the tides, producing dangerously brackish water. The tidal movement did not make the river a good location for a mill. More importantly, with its head only a few miles inland, the Mystic did not go anywhere in particular. The river served better as a protected cove or small bay for any farms that the colonists might develop near its shores. The land stretching for fifteen miles in either direction of the Mystic River, however, would remain just as contested under colonial occupation as it had under the Pequot.

The villages at the Mystic River would grow from the towns that developed on the more important Thames and Pawcatuck Rivers to the east and west. The Thames River, the more valued of the two, was wide, deep and provided a path far inland. The Pawcatuck River also provided a navigable waterway into the interior and lay on the border of Narragansett territory. Any town founded there would have access to their trade. The path taken by John Mason's expedition against the Pequot connected the two rivers . This trail, called the Pequot Trail, ran northwest from a narrow point on the Pawcatuck to the head of the Mystic River, where travelers could wade across the water, then proceeded overland to the Thames. The Pequot Trail would be instrumental in the development of the second Mystic village (the first of European origin).

The colonial migration that spawned that first European Mystic village began in the 1640s, when the General Court at Hartford began surveying and granting land in the conquered Pequot territory to Pequot War veterans from the Connecticut River settlements. Within three years, John Winthrop Jr., son of the governor of Massachusetts Bay Colony, founded Pequot Plantation near the mouth of the Thames River at the behest of the Massachusetts Bay Colony. Those brave enough to venture

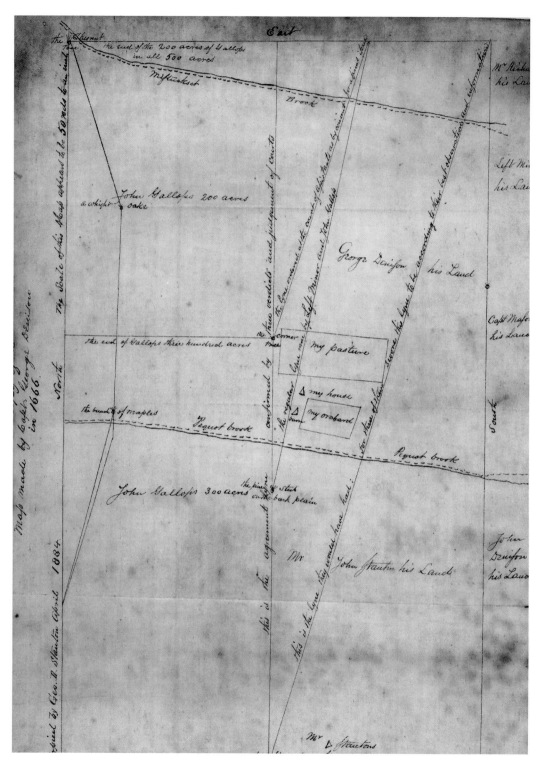

This 1884 copy of a 1666 map shows the first English land claims in Stonington on the eastern banks of the Mystic River. Notations for boundaries include one beginning at a wooden stick. *Stonington Historical Society.*

to this remote village would receive both a town lot and farm acreage somewhere in the surrounding vicinity. Many of the first settlers were veterans of the Pequot War who had served under the leadership of Massachusetts Bay officers.

These earliest white migrants to the region included William Chesebrough and Thomas Stanton, a couple of individualists who preferred to conduct business at the far reaches of colonial settlement. William Chesebrough had several run-ins with authorities in England, Massachusetts Bay and Plymouth. This prompted his migration to Pequot Plantation, which he also found not to his liking. In 1644, as he returned to Massachusetts with his family, he passed a small cove lying between the Mystic and Pawcatuck Rivers and decided to settle there. At this cove, called Wequetequock, he established a trading post and farm. Even this far from colonial authorities, Chesebrough continued to find himself under suspicion of trading firearms and alcohol to the Native Americans, the former of which had been outlawed by the Connecticut General Court in 1644.

Thomas Stanton, the interpreter in Mason's forces during the war and an experienced and successful trader, received both land and a five-year monopoly on trade with all Native American tribes on the Pawcatuck River. In 1650, he and his family founded a trading post along the river, near a common crossing point but with water deep enough to dock a coastal trading vessel. He and Chesebrough were the first two permanent English settlers in the territory that became the town of Stonington.

Yet settlement east of the Thames River proceeded slowly in the first two decades after the Pequot War. The territory itself was quite dangerous. The elimination of the Pequot had left a power vacuum among the remaining Native American nations. The Narragansett, led by Miantonomo, dominated the surrounding tribes and lay claim to the former Pequot territory from the Thames to the Pawcatuck. While the colonists claimed ownership of that land by right of conquest, they continued to negotiate with local villages for the purchase of the land, and the Narragansett intended to control and benefit from that arrangement. The Mohegan, led by Uncas, had different ideas. His alliance with the Narragansett had been one of convenience. Uncas claimed the former Pequot territory for the Mohegan. The ensuing war between these two nations resulted in the death of Miantonomo and an ostensible Mohegan victory, but from 1643 to 1644, anyone venturing into the disputed land might find themselves caught between two war parties.

Additionally, England and the Netherlands went to war with one another over colonial claims four times between 1652 and 1784. In the New England colonies, these wars inevitably drew in allied Native American nations. Already, the General Court of Connecticut had trouble with the Dutch traders to the west. They attempted to negotiate a boundary between Dutch and English territory in the 1650 Treaty of Hartford. As with many borders drawn through the wilderness, this one was largely ignored in practice. Meanwhile, the Narragansett continued their trading partnership with the Dutch, allowing armed Dutch vessels to anchor in the Narragansett Bay. When war broke out in 1652, Connecticut again raised a militia, led by John Mason, to carry out short expeditions against the Narragansett, and settlement around the Mystic River became a dangerous prospect for two years.

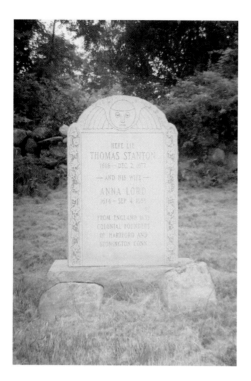

This twenty-first-century headstone stands in Wequetequock burial ground, the oldest in Stonington, over the graves of Thomas Stanton and his wife, Anna. Stanton, who had participated in the Pequot War as an interpreter, became a trader to the Narragansett and Pequot survivors. *Photo by author, 2006.*

Territorial disputes between the Connecticut and Massachusetts Bay governments also stalled European migration to the Mystic River. In the 1640s and 1650s, "Connecticut" referred to settlements along the Connecticut River, and its claim to any other land existed primarily on paper. Several different governing bodies might lay claim to the same place. As long as the land remained unused by any of those bodies, the conflict was essentially theoretical. When settlers began moving onto that land, however, problems arose.

While Connecticut held no royal charter separating it from the Massachusetts Bay Colony, its remote location had granted it significant independence. The towns that composed Connecticut went so far as to create their own government to meet the crises that arose with the Pequot War, and they maintained that government afterward in order to manage local matters including land grants and Native American relations. The Pequot War represented the convergence of these two issues. The Pequot had presented an immediate problem. The leaders of the settlements banded together and formed a General Court to deal with this problem, which led to the expedition against the Pequot. After the Pequot War, the court claimed the Pequot land by right of conquest as a means to pay the Connecticut soldiers.

The Massachusetts Bay Colony saw the situation differently. The Massachusetts Bay militia had participated in the war by sending companies under John Underhill and Captain Thomas Stoughton. Massachusetts Bay forces had also patrolled the coast for some months before the war, searching for the killers of John Stone and John Oldham.

Since Massachusetts Bay legally claimed Connecticut, its government considered its own authority, including the right to distribute the Pequot land, as superseding that of the Connecticut General Court. Hence, John Winthrop Jr. founded Pequot Plantation on the Thames River as an outpost for his father's colony, answerable to the Bay Colony rather than the Connecticut Court.

In 1646, the very existence of Pequot Plantation forced the two colonies to turn to the United Colonies of New England to resolve their competing claims. The United Colonies of New England had been formed in 1643 as a confederation of Connecticut, Massachusetts Bay and Plymouth, in order to peacefully solve such disputes as this. The commissioners of the United Colonies voted to place the boundary between the claims of Massachusetts Bay and Connecticut at the Thames River. Connecticut would lie west of the river and Massachusetts Bay could claim the land to the east, including the Mystic River.

With the war between the Narragansett and Mohegan over, and with the boundary between the claims of Massachusetts Bay and Connecticut set, settlers began to appear in the land around the Mystic River throughout the next decade. John Mason, who had led the colonists against the Pequot, had already been granted five hundred acres on the eastern banks of the Mystic River, as well as the island that later bore his name, although he never lived on the land. In 1653, John Gallup Jr., the son of the captain of the ship that had found John Oldham's body before the Pequot War, received three hundred acres about halfway up the east side of the river. There, he carved a depression into a rocky hill overlooking the river. Many early settlers did this, using the dugout as the cellar for the larger house they would eventually build on the same site. The fact that Gallup built a wall around his little man-made cave suggests that he still considered the area quite dangerous, the threat coming from wild animals hunting his livestock if not from the ever-shifting human allegiances of this backcountry.

Other settlers joined Gallup within the year. Thomas Miner, who had immigrated to Massachusetts with John Winthrop's party in 1630, was granted several plots, the main one lying on Quiambaug Cove, east of the Mystic River. In 1654, George Denison, an English Civil War veteran of Oliver Cromwell's army, received his own tract of three hundred acres, just south of Gallup's piece, on the west side of the river. Robert Park purchased his own plot north of Gallup's farm. The Reverend Robert Blinman, who had led a group of settlers from Gloucester to New London, as well as the Beebe brothers, Thomas Parke and Connecticut Governor John Hayne, also received grants. Like Captain John Mason, not all of these men lived on their land. Many sold it for an increased price or hired an overseer to work the land. Most, however, brought their wives and children, indicating their intention to form a community in the Mystic River Valley.

One woman did not arrive as a wife, however. Massachusetts Bay had also granted land to Margaret Lake, a widow and the only woman to receive such a grant in her own name. Socially and economically, however, Lake resembled many of her male compatriots, who were all closely tied to the existing and rising leadership of Massachusetts Bay. Her sister was married to Massachusetts Bay Governor John Winthrop, and her daughter was married to John Gallup. Like many of the men, Lake also did not live on her land, but took up residence in Pequot Plantation and hired overseers to manage her property.

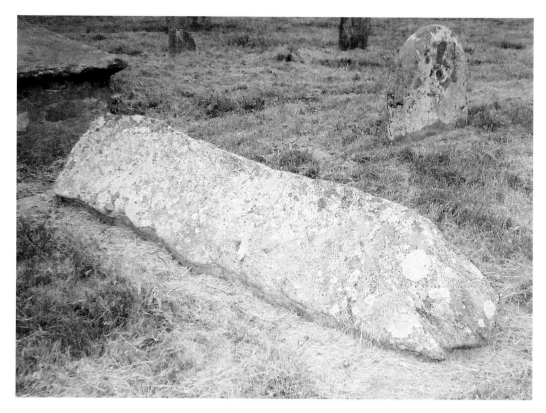

"Wolfstones" were supposed to protect graves from being exhumed by packs of wolves. Wolves also threatened livestock, resulting in annual mass hunts by colonists that contributed to the extermination of the wolf population by the 1800s. *Photo by author, 2006.*

One grantee who did live on his farm, James Morgan, also found that he would have to negotiate the daily terms of use of his land with a small band of Native Americans led by their sachem, Robin Cassacinamon. This small remnant of the Pequot lived on the east side of the river, near its mouth and adjacent to the land of both Morgan and John Mason. Both Native Americans and colonists tended to allow their livestock to roam freely during the day to forage on undergrowth. Unfortunately, this often led to the crops of both parties being eaten as feed, and the livestock being hunted as game. Cassacinamon was not in a position to dispute Morgan and Mason when they insisted that the Pequot refrain from harming the English livestock and take responsibility for damages that their own livestock committed on English crops.

Controlling livestock, however, was not so easily accomplished. An ear of corn eaten by a cow or a foraging pig resulted in the animal being shot like a deer and held the potential for violent retaliation or, at the very least, led to frequent and incessant negotiations and reparations. In 1666, when Cassacinamon appealed to the General Court for relief, the court's solution was to remove the Pequot village to a more remote location farther north of the Mystic River. Not surprisingly, this land was not particularly coveted by English settlers. Cassacinamon and his village, and in turn their descendants, slowly and reluctantly moved to the reservation over the next century.

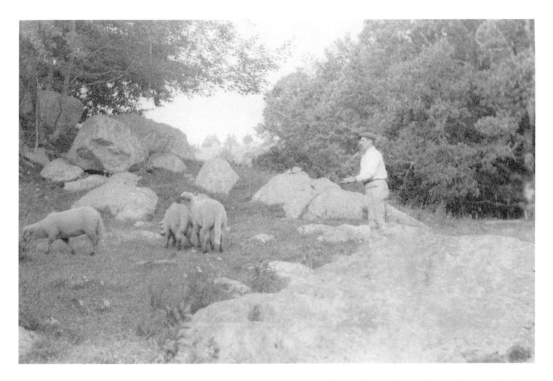

From the colonial era, the wool of Mystic sheep supplied its mills and weavers, and textiles remained an important part of the local economy into the twentieth century. *Photo from Indian and Colonial Research Center, Inc., Old Mystic, Connecticut.*

If the conflict with the Native Americans had temporarily abated near the Mystic River, conflict between the colonies had just begun. Massachusetts Bay had the authority to grant land east of the Thames River, and many of the settlers hailed from that colony; but the Connecticut General Court did not discourage people from claiming the land that it had granted, particularly between the Mystic and Pawcatuck Rivers. Thus, the population was a mix of people whose rights to land was granted by two different entities. Those who received grants from Massachusetts did not recognize the legality of grants made by Connecticut, and those who had received grants from Connecticut before Massachusetts Bay had exerted its authority over the land would not relinquish their farms to Massachusetts Bay. Thomas Miner represented the opinion of the latter group when he wrote in his diary, "Because that the bay men begun in an unjust way to lay out mens lands that they had in possession before the things were wholly ended makes me to turn wholly to Coneticut [*sic*]." The problem, which lay dormant for several years, reached a crisis point when the settlers in that area petitioned for the designation of a town.

The main unit of local governance in Massachusetts Bay and Connecticut was the town. The town centered on the church and the town council, and the law required church attendance. As devout Puritans, each member believed that church attendance was necessary not only for the salvation of their own soul, but for the community as well. Yet neither town nor church was permitted without the approval of the colony's government.

In the 1650s, all of the land east of the Thames River was considered part of the town of Pequot Plantation, and all of the people living under the jurisdiction of Pequot Plantation were required to attend that church every Sunday. The farther away a person lived from the town center, the more difficult travel on Sunday became. The few roads were little more than dirt paths through the woods, which were covered with snow in the winter. Those settlers living between the Mystic and the Pawcatuck Rivers not only had the farthest distance to travel, but they also had to overcome the obstacle of the Mystic River itself. Thus, in 1654, they sent a petition to the General Court of Connecticut to form their own congregation. While the church issue was their main concern, they may have also wanted an organized decision-making body that would have the authority to respond quickly to local problems involving defense and roads.

The Connecticut Court refused their petition in 1654 and again in May 1657. Then, in October 1657, a group of residents organized by George Denison, Walter Palmer, William Thompson and Thomas Stanton appealed to an authority outside of Connecticut by sending a petition requesting the intervention of Massachusetts Bay. The Massachusetts Bay government, hoping to wrest control of this corner of the colony away from Connecticut, happily assisted. As under the Pequot, the land between the Thames and Pawcatuck Rivers remained strategically located, with two rivers reaching inland to better farming territory, borders providing access to Native American trade and a southern coast that would provide ports for trade farther down the seaboard to the West Indies.

For the next year, the matter of the area that was by then being called the Pawcatuck territory bounced among colonial authorities. Massachusetts Bay took up the matter of Pawcatuck with the General Court at Hartford, claiming the land as part of Massachusetts Bay on the basis of the agreements made in the wake of the Pequot War as well as by right of conquest. The Connecticut General Court also claimed the territory by right of conquest. When the two bodies reached an impasse, the dispute moved to the United Colonies of New England. There the matter was debated for five months.

Meanwhile, the residents of the Pawcatuck territory lived in legal limbo. Denison, Stanton and Palmer, along with eight other men and the consent of Massachusetts Bay, attempted to remedy the situation by creating the Association of Pawcatuck People. They alluded to lawlessness in their neighborhood, declaring "thear hath bene injurious insolencys done unto soom persons," citing specifically "the cattell of others threatened to be taken away,—and the chattel of soom others already taken away by violence." In the interest of public safety and "the better to confirm a mutual confidence in one another and that we may be preserved in righteousness and peac with such as do commerce with us," they had formed their own local governing body and reserved for themselves the right to issue warrants, make arrests, hear and judge court cases and punish criminals. They may have also hoped to use it as a tool to establish their own local authority.

The Association of Pawcatuck People did not speak for all settlers in the Pawcatuck territory. Supporters of the Massachusetts Bay faction apprehended Thomas Miner, who had made his support of the Connecticut claim known. They accused him of leading the opposition against Denison and Stanton, plotting to overthrow Denison as a leader of the community by delivering him to Connecticut authorities and "lightnes at Towne." He was released unharmed but warned.

In October 1658, the commissioners of the United Colonies of New England made their decision. The Mystic River would divide Massachusetts Bay and Connecticut. The Pawcatuck territory would fall to Massachusetts Bay and assume the name Southington. Not surprisingly, the signers of the Association of Pawcatuck People's declaration became the leaders of Southington and the surveyors of its boundaries. George Denison, in particular, held several powerful positions, including those of militia captain and court commissioner.

Yet the territorial disputes did not end. Colonists from Rhode Island had begun purchasing land from various Narragansett and former Pequot tribes inside of Southington's borders, while Connecticut colonists continued to claim parts of Southington as their own. On two occasions, John Mason appealed to the United Colonies on behalf of the Connecticut General Court, requesting that they return Southington to Connecticut, but to no avail. As Connecticut and Rhode Island colonists moved into Southington, the town officials begged the Massachusetts government to intervene.

Connecticut Governor John Winthrop Jr., however, circumvented all colonial authorities. In 1662, he sailed to England and obtained a royal charter from Charles II. This charter officially established Connecticut as a separate colony from Massachusetts Bay. This charter also set the eastern boundary at Narragansett Bay, placing Southington back inside the borders of Connecticut. Rhode Island disputed this charter, and after much negotiation, the boundary between the two colonies was set at the Pawcatuck River in 1663.

Southington had become part of Connecticut. Some leaders of the Massachusetts Bay faction resisted this change, most notably George Denison, who was arrested at one point for continuing to exercise the authority to perform marriages as given to him by Massachusetts, but most accepted the new jurisdiction. In 1665, the town was renamed Mystic in tribute to the settlers who were veterans of the Pequot War. Less than a year later, the name was again changed, this time to Stonington, supposedly in reference to the rocky soil noted by both inhabitants and travelers alike. By the 1670s, boundary disputes between the colonies over the land east of the Mystic River had ceased.

By 1675, the population of New England had shifted dramatically. English immigration had peaked during the Great Migration of the 1640s, but dropped during the English Commonwealth and Protectorate of the 1650s, only to surge again after the restoration of the Stuart monarchy. At the same time, the Great Migration immigrants had produced large families who were entering adulthood by the 1670s. This combination of immigration and high rates of fertility had led to a booming population demanding more land farther from established population centers. This translated into an aggressive attitude toward the Native American tribes who inhabited that land.

At the same time, the Native American population had declined rapidly. Rampant epidemics hit every tribe, and fur-bearing animals that also served as food had disappeared with the growth of the fur trade and English farming. Surviving tribes banded together less for gaining advantage against the colonists than for survival. As with the English population, a younger generation had reached adulthood. This generation saw less advantage in courting the English as allies, and displayed more hostility toward English negotiators and settlements.

Metacom, known to the English as "King Philip," was a prime example of this generational shift. His father, Massasoit, had seen an advantage to cultivating amicable relations with the Pilgrims when they had landed at Plymouth fifty years earlier. After his death, his older son, Wamsutta, had plotted against the Plymouth Colony and met with a questionable end. Metacom, Massasoit's younger son, became sachem and planned an attack on English settlements throughout New England. His plan was exposed by one of his translators, who was summarily executed by the Wampanoag. The executors were, in turn, executed by the English in Massachusetts. In retaliation, in June 1675, Metacom ordered an attack on the English village at Swansea on the eastern shore of Narragansett Bay, and began King Philip's War against Plymouth and Massachusetts Bay.

The Wampanoag attack on Swansea alarmed all colonists from Narragansett Bay to the Thames River. Swansea lay less than one hundred miles from the Mystic River, and the Narragansett territory lay just over the Pawcatuck River. The colonists' former alliance with the Narragansett had deteriorated in the previous decades, and many believed that if the Narragansett nation allied with the Wampanoag, an attack on the villages in the Mystic River Valley would surely follow. The United Colonies rushed to secure the neutrality of the Narragansett. Nonetheless, as news arrived of the attacks along the upper Connecticut River, the residents of Stonington and Pequot Plantation, now called "New London," expected an immediate attack and began to fortify their villages.

Yet the Narragansett also controlled a valuable and sizeable chunk of land that bordered on the colony, and the frequent negotiations for their neutrality were a constant annoyance to the colonists. Additionally, in August 1675, a great storm, possibly a hurricane, hit southern New England. The coast between the Connecticut River and Cape Cod bore the greatest brunt of this storm. According to Puritan belief, such ill fortune as both war and a natural disaster were afflictions sent by God to punish a sinful colony. If the Native Americans were the devil incarnate in the Puritans' eyes, then their elimination would represent an act of profound Christian devotion. War with the Narragansett, as with the Pequot forty years earlier, would also present the perfect opportunity to eliminate them as a threat and open their land for English settlement.

To that end, the Connecticut Court raised a militia under the command of John Mason's son, John Mason Jr., while local forces at Stonington and New London organized under John Gallup Jr., Thomas Miner and James Avery. In December 1675, the Stonington and New London forces combined and launched an assault into the Narragansett territory. They attacked the Narragansett in an area near Kingston, Rhode Island, called the Great Swamp. In the ensuing battle, the Connecticut colonists killed three hundred Native Americans, while losing only eighty of their own men, including John Gallup Jr. and John Mason Jr. Similar incursions into Narragansett territory, conducted by the militia from Stonington and New London, continued until the war's end in August 1676, when Massachusetts forces killed Metacom. While the end of King Philip's War did not end the hostile relationship between Native Americans and New England colonists, it did eliminate the Narragansett threat to the settlements in southeastern Connecticut, including those around the Mystic River.

With the end of the border disputes and the Narragansett threat, the population of the Mystic River Valley grew rapidly, and the infrastructure and economy to support and encourage greater settlement began to develop. The Pequot Trail was the main highway around the Mystic River, and it became instrumental in the growth of settlement at the river's head. Access to the trail was crucial for all landholders in the area, allowing them to transport livestock, crops, equipment and manufactured goods to and from their farms. Additionally, the major landholders often held local and colonial offices, which required them to travel out of the region. The land granted to the veterans of the Pequot War abutted either the trail or the shore. Gallup and Denison, the earliest settlers, had access to both. Those, such as Miner and the Masons, whose land adjoined the shore, ensured that smaller roads were built to connect their land to the Pequot Trail.

A desire to connect to the Pequot Trail was not limited to the settlers on the east side of the river, but landholders on the west side of the river had a more difficult time reaching the trail. There, settlement had spread east from the Thames River into the Poquonnock plains, a flat area of land near the shore and between the granite ridges that rose above the banks of the Mystic and the Thames Rivers. Since most of the Poquonnock landholders lived in New London, a road had been built from Cary Latham's ferry on the Thames River into the farmland, but no farther. The settlers on the west bank of the Mystic River—including the Beebes at the mouth of the river, the Packers and the Parkes—lay closer to the Pequot Trail to their north, which could be reached by a road that skirted the western bank of the river. The shortest route to the trail traveling east, however, crossed the Mystic River.

As early as 1660, Robert Burrows had received permission to establish a ferry somewhere along the middle of the length of the river, earning his home the name of Half-way House. Tradition holds that the ferry crossed at a point near where the I-95 bridge was built in the twentieth century. This would have connected the path that ran along the western bank of the river to John Gallup's farm on the east side of the river. The ferry may have also crossed the river farther to the south, closer to the point where, a century later, the Packer family ran a ferry. The latter is more likely, as most of the farms on the west side of the river lay closer to its mouth, and a trail from the ferry would have had only a short distance to go before it connected with the one crossing the Denison property and heading toward the Pequot Trail.

In addition to connecting farms to the markets, the Pequot Trail connected these Puritan settlers to their church. One of the main issues that led to the creation of the town of Stonington had been the difficulty that the Stonington residents encountered in traveling to church. When the town of Stonington was granted leave to build its own church, members chose a location on the trail partway between the settlement on the Mystic and the Pawcatuck Rivers. The structure became known as the Road

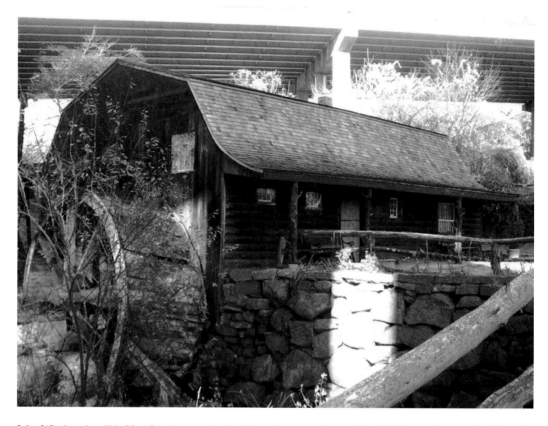

John Winthrop's mill in New London was the first in southeastern Connecticut. Winthrop also owned mills at the head of the Mystic River. Seen here in a 2006 photograph, the mill sits near its original site, now located under the I-95 bridge over the Thames River. *Photo by author, 2006.*

Church. As the religious community around the Mystic River grew and diversified, new churches were built in the village along the trail at the head of the river.

The church was not the only civic institution to arise in Mystic. In 1679, John Fish became the first schoolmaster in Stonington. Education was of primary importance in the New England colonies, with Massachusetts being the first colony to require towns of fifty families or more to provide public elementary education for their children. Even girls and African and Native American servants or slaves were allowed basic literacy skills. Most New England families had six or more children, and as the adult population of Mystic grew, the number of children grew more rapidly. Fish probably had a sizable class for the location and conducted lessons in his home near the growing village at the head of the river.

Fish also provides insight into some of the laws governing marriage in Mystic at the time. He had been granted ten acres of land on the east side of the river in 1668, to which he brought his wife. Five years later, however, she ran off with Samuel Culver. Divorce was not common and was seldom granted in the Puritan-dominated colonies. A deserted spouse could only file for divorce after six years had passed, thus proving that the fugitive spouse was truly gone. Fish was finally able to obtain his divorce in

1680. His status as a deserted husband and divorced man, however, did not seem to sully his reputation with the community, as the locals continued to allow him to educate their offspring.

Meanwhile, businesses began to develop at the intersection of the Pequot Trail and the Mystic River. In 1664, Edward Culver, father of Samuel, had been granted a small piece of land at that point and built a tavern for the use of travelers on the trail. In 1674, John Winthrop Jr., who lived in New London, bought land along one of the brooks that spilled into the Mystic, and he had a gristmill built there. John Lamb ran the mill for Winthrop, whom he persuaded to also build a fulling mill. The gristmill attracted farmers from both sides of the river, who brought their grain to Mystic for grinding. The fulling mill, which would clean the oils and dirt from woven cloth, brought in the goods of local shepherds and weavers. One of the patrons of this fulling mill was most certainly William Gallup, son of John Gallup. He, or more likely his wife, possessed not only a spinning wheel, but also a loom by 1680. Big, bulky pieces of equipment, looms were not common household items, and women who owned and used them tended to weave cloth for most of their neighbors. Additionally, a sawmill soon appeared, which turned the seemingly endless supply of trees into suitable building material for homes, wagons and watercraft. A blacksmith shop kept livestock shod and manufactured and repaired metal objects used in cooking, building and hunting. By 1700, an industrious village was taking shape at the head of the river.

Through the seventeenth century, both as part of the Pequot dominion and then as an English colony, the Mystic River lay in a strategic location. In and of itself, the river was not useful for trade or transportation at that point in its history. Nonetheless, the river occupied territory between the important locations of the Thames and Pawcatuck Rivers locally and the Narragansett Bay and Connecticut River regionally. The river also occupied territory between competing populations, both native and colonial. As such, the land surrounding it became hotly contested and its inhabitants were drawn into armed conflict. Yet after the Pequot War, the land was only threatened, but not directly attacked or invaded. The European settlers may have fortified their homes and marched off to war in the adjoining country, but on their own land, they fought more among themselves. Thus, the small village of Mystic was slowly able to form as the seventeenth century drew to a close.

CHAPTER 3

THE VILLAGES AND THE ATLANTIC WORLD, 1700–1815

With the Native Americans all but eliminated as a threat, and the inter-colonial border disputes settled so far as the Mystic River was concerned, its surrounding land ceased to hold strategic political value for greater, competing colonial interests. Instead, the three villages that grew along the banks of the Mystic River became peripheral to the action shaping the American nation during the period of colonial wars—including the American Revolution and the War of 1812—and developed the character of a farming community. As Newport to the east and New York and New London to the west became important centers of commerce, the Mystic River villages benefited from their locations between these cities and at the easternmost end of Long Island Sound. At the same time, the nearly impassable roads and limited navigation of the river deflected potentially hostile attention away from the villages, allowing them to survive the destruction visited upon more strategic towns and cities, and provided a safe haven for those fleeing that destruction.

By the first decade of the eighteenth century, three villages had begun to develop along the Mystic River. The largest village, called Mystic, also known as Head of the River, lay at that eponymous location where several creeks converged into the Mystic River estuary. Here, the leg of the Boston Post Road between Providence and New London passed. Two villages also lay farther down the river, although to call them "villages" might seem more than generous. One lay on the eastern side of the river, in the town that was called Stonington after 1665. This village was called Lower Mystic, and consisted of only twelve houses by the early 1800s. These houses lay along Willow Street, which ended at the ferry landing. On the opposite bank of the river, in the town of Groton, stood the village that became known as Portersville.

Through the eighteenth century, Mystic's economic foundations would begin in these three villages. The international wars that drove European global diplomacy would propel Mystic's development beyond its local region and draw its residents into

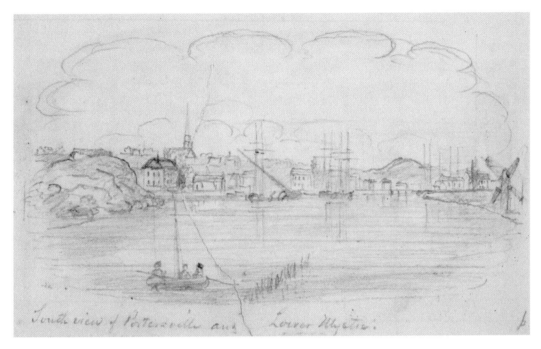

The earliest view of the villages on the lower Mystic River, drawn by John Warner Barber in 1836, shows shipbuilding, windmills and an early wooden bridge. *John Warner Barber Collection, Graphics Collection, Connecticut Historical Society.*

the major events of the Atlantic world. The three major components of this economy would be manufacturing, roads and maritime trades.

Agriculture lay at the heart of the colonial economy, and the overwhelming majority of colonists in America were farmers. Indeed, as far as the English government was concerned, one main function of the colonies was to provide England with the raw material resources that would feed its emerging system of manufacturing. The role of settlers in the Mystic River Valley did not differ from this pattern. Land was the source of wealth, and the land along the river drew the first settlers.

The rocky soil around the Mystic River prevented the early farmers in the area from producing cash crops. But this did not necessarily lead to poverty. Farmers grew grain, corn, peas, potatoes and fruit. They raised cattle, pigs, chicken and sheep. They hunted and fished and maintained wood stores and salt marshes. If well situated, a farm could become quite prosperous. These farms were generally maintained and supported by the families who lived on them, and New England families tended to grow rather large, with an average of nine children, who provided the labor. When a farmer required more labor, he turned to indentured servants or slave labor. By the end of the seventeenth century, Connecticut farmers were sending marketable produce and livestock in huge numbers to the West Indies.

New England was inextricably tied to the slave trade throughout the colonial era, with some of the largest slave markets and investors in the slave trade living in Rhode Island.

The demand for slave labor itself, however, was small and kept the black population at approximately 3 percent of the total population. Of the total black population in New England, the largest numbers lived in Connecticut. Although New London County had one of the highest concentrations of African Americans, the towns of Groton and Stonington had few black residents, and enslaved people appeared individually or as small families in the households of the more prominent farmers. With so little dependence upon slave labor in general, the gradual emancipation act passed by the State of Connecticut in 1794 caused no great outcry.

The most famous enslaved man in the vicinity of Mystic was Venture Smith, whose narrative was published in 1798. As a small child, he had been captured in Africa and sold to slave traders from Rhode Island. He was owned by and hired out to a series of masters in Connecticut, including Thomas Stanton, a direct descendant of the Pequot translator and trader, and Hempsted Miner, both of whom lived in Stonington. Another owner was Colonel Oliver Smith, who was a shipbuilder in Mystic. It is through this Mystic owner that Smith received his last name. He was eventually sold to a master in Hartford, and then moved to East Haddam, but his story provides insight into the vagaries and opportunities for African Americans in southeastern Connecticut. He suffered both abuse and discrimination, yet also was able to purchase his freedom and that of his family, own land and operate a shipping business. His experience suggests the general ambivalence that white New Englanders felt toward slavery and racial equality, permitting slaves to read and write, yet forbidding black people from voting or serving in the militia.

Agriculture in Mystic did not require a large supply of labor, which precluded the widespread use of slaves. In turn, that prevented racial diversity. At the same time, subsistence farming did open opportunities for economic diversity. Even subsistence crops required some form of processing to become useful. Corn and other grains had to be ground into meal and flour. Cattle hides had to be tanned to become leather. Apples had to be turned into cider. Sheep wool had to be spun and woven to become cloth. Manufacturing in Mystic emerged early, with the growth of mills to support local agriculture. The closer to home that this conversion took place, the less expensive the process. Thus, those of an entrepreneurial spirit did well to enter a farming community and set up a mill that catered to one of these markets.

In Mystic, John Winthrop Jr. had opened the earliest of these mills. John Lamb ran this gristmill for Winthrop along one of the creeks that fed into the Mystic River. By 1700, three additional gristmills operated on the Groton side of the river. In 1712, Robert Burrows also built a gristmill, which he sold to Thomas Chipman in 1725. At the turn of the eighteenth century, Stephen Avery also owned a gristmill, which he sold to John Hyde in the early nineteenth century. Fewer gristmills appeared in Lower Mystic on the eastern side of the river, but an etching dating from the 1830s shows a windmill on Pistol Point, suggesting that mills did eventually develop on that side of the river as well. This was the mill of Ebenezer Beebe. The head of the river, however, provided a more logical point for the development of mills, due both to the slight elevation change (providing greater motion for water to power the mills) and the Boston Post Road that ran across the river at that point, providing farmers transportation to the mill.

Lamb soon saw the opportunities for other types of mills when he opened a fulling mill. At that time, much textile manufacturing took place in private homes. Most women, particularly single women, found a good deal of their time consumed by spinning. Weaving required larger pieces of equipment and greater skill, and therefore centralized the labor with the individual woman or itinerant weaver who owned the loom. Fabric, however, required a cleaning and strengthening step that called for a greater investment of resources in large quantities of urine, special clay, soap and water. Again, centralized labor was more efficient for this process of fulling.

Six years later, William Gallup added his own loom and several spinning wheels to this local textile industry, and in 1700, James Dean Jr. opened another fulling mill to the east of the river. In 1725, Chipman opened another fulling mill at Head of the River, and he identified himself as a "clothier" in tax records, implying more diverse production. Between 1812 and 1814, anticipating a boom in textiles after the War of 1812, gristmill owner John Hyde opened a cotton mill at Head of the River, which became the basis for his Mystic Manufacturing Company. Although two-thirds of national textile manufacturing was still taking place in private residences in 1810, these early inroads provided the basis for later Mystic businesses to expand and diversify, and textile manufacturing would have the longest life of any other industry along the Mystic River.

Other manufacturing opportunities presented themselves in the natural resources of the region. Two saltworks, which were key to preservation of meat, operated along the Mystic River by 1776. Stephen Wilcox ran one, just north of Pistol Point, and another lay farther up the river at Adams Point. A third appeared on Groton Long Point, near the mouth of the river, around the time of the American Revolution. Timber, however, was a greater resource, and one of the main attractions of the American colonies for the English government was its supply of timber for fuel, construction and naval stores. In fact, this hunger for wood would lead to the almost total deforestation of Stonington and Groton by the early nineteenth century. A sawmill was already operating on the western bank of the Mystic River in 1700, and in 1766 Samuel Gallup opened one on the Stonington side along Mixtuxet Brook. John Hyde, already the owner of a gristmill and a cotton mill, opened a sawmill at Head of the River sometime around 1813. While lumber manufacturing did not become, in and of itself, central to Mystic's economy, it was a constant and important source for construction in the area, particularly in shipbuilding.

In the eighteenth century, Mystic's manufacturing supported local agriculture and formed the basis for later growth in the nineteenth century. This manufacturing also supported, and was supported by, road building through Stonington and Groton. The three villages on the river became the foci for a sunburst of roads connecting the villages to one another and to towns farther away, all of which aided the continued growth of Mystic.

During this time, overland travel was harsh and inefficient. When Sarah Kemble Knight passed through Stonington in 1704, she noted the rocky and perilous path, writing, "I Ridd on very slowly thro' Stoningtown, where the Rode was very stony and

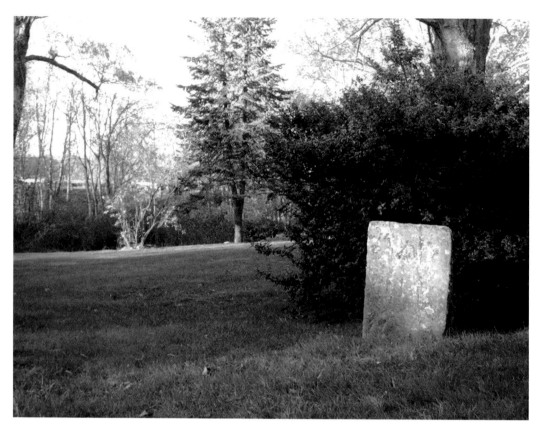

Mile marker seven sat on the Old Boston Post Road. In the background runs Connecticut State Highway 184, which replaced the Post Road in the 1920s. The number seven indicated the distance in miles to New London. *Photo by author, 2006.*

uneven." Dr. Alexander Hamilton, forty years later, reported that conditions had not improved, writing in his journal that he "rode eight miles thro a very stonny rough road where the stones upon each hand of us seemed as large as houses, and the way itself a mere rock." He added, "This is properly enough called Stonnington [*sic*]." The expense of improvements meant that most road building resulted from community effort, cooperative effort between communities or a higher governmental body. As such, throughout the history of road building in the region, roads followed well-worn paths, bound communities to one another and invested the villages of Mystic in the operations of state and national governments.

Knight and Hamilton, as well as many sojourners before and after, traveled along the major highway of colonial New England: the Boston Post Road. This road had three branches, the southernmost of which led from Boston to New York, passing through Providence, New London and New Haven. The stretch that ran from Westerly, Rhode Island, through Stonington to the head of the Mystic River, followed the Pequot Trail. This path continued on toward the Thames River, cutting through the northern part of Groton and crossing the river at the ferry in the village of Groton Bank.

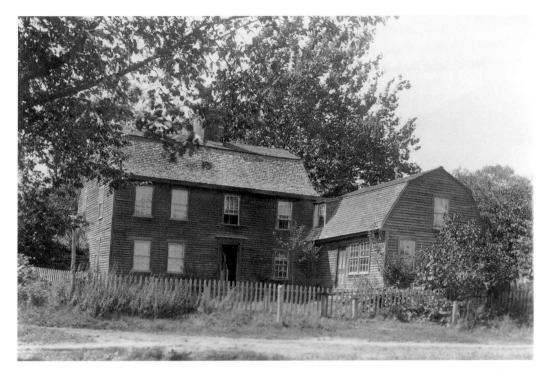

The John Burrows house, also known as the Woodbridge Tavern, sits at the center of Old Mystic and served travelers on the Boston Post Road, which ran to the left of this image. *Photo from Indian and Colonial Research Center, Inc., Old Mystic, Connecticut.*

In 1751, Benjamin Franklin, who was then a deputy postmaster of the English government, set out to survey and measure the existing Post Road in New England. Riding in a specially designed carriage and using a primitive odometer, Franklin's expedition carefully marked each mile along the road. In 1818, however, Westerly was cut off from the Post Road when it was resurveyed as part of the Groton and Stonington Turnpike between the Thames and Pawcatuck Rivers. This new path between Hopkinton, Rhode Island, and Mystic was incorporated into the Post Road and became the new route for stagecoaches, excluding the Old Pequot Trail. The trail, however, remained important to transportation and communication in the region.

Other paths leading to Head of the River village lent to its local importance as a crossroads. In 1660, a road was built connecting the Mystic River to Norwich, north of New London on the Thames River. Another road led to the farmland at Lantern Hill to the northeast. These two roads converged with the Boston Post Road at Head of the River. Thus, this Mystic village became an attractive location, with roads leading north, east and west and a waterway leading south, thereby prompting the farmers and manufacturers in the surrounding area to connect their farms to the village through their own road building efforts.

On the eastern side of the river, the Lower Mystic village focused its earliest road building on the goal of eliminating as many miles as possible from the overland journeys to Providence and Boston. In 1721, Willow Street was laid out from the ferry landing on Pistol Point to the foot of Slaughterhouse Hill. This road connected the ferry to farms between the river and the Old Pequot Trail. In 1729, Willow Street was extended over the hill, connecting with another road leading from Masons Island and intersecting with the Post Road. In 1760, another road connected Pistol Point to the Pequot Trail at Head of the River, providing villagers with access to points farther north and east. An added benefit was the shorter journey to the closest Congregational church.

On the western side of the river, the Poquonnock plain remained connected by road only to the Thames River. In 1709, a road was surveyed through the granite ridge lying between the Mystic River and the plain. This road connected Fort Hill, on the eastern edge of Poquonnock, to the ferry run by the Packer family on the Mystic River where the Mystic village of Portersville was growing. This road was later known as the New London Road. Another path followed the western bank of the river, connecting Portersville with the fishing village of Noank farther south and Head of the River to the north. The road to Head of the River proved much more problematic because it ran through marshes at the foot of rocky hills. A better road appeared along the ridge of these hills leading from the New London Road to the Post Road.

Attendant to these roads grew the earliest vestiges of a hospitality industry in the form of taverns to support the post riders and, after 1732, stagecoach travelers. In 1745, Dr. Dudley Woodbridge built one of the earliest of these establishments at the crossroads of the three major highways that converged at Head of the River. Others appeared on the Old Pequot Trail near the Road Church and on the road toward Groton. Taverns were not only resting spots, but along with the churches and meetinghouses, they became places of congregation for village citizens. While the churches and meetinghouses served formal functions—ministering to people in a larger geographical area and influenced by higher institutional authorities—taverns allowed informal gatherings of local people free from any direct institutional control beyond that of the tavern keeper yet immediately connected to the outside world by passing messengers.

Despite the growth in the number and mileage of roads, overland travel did not improve in quality until the nineteenth century, due to the lack of available funds and road building technology. Most roads were merely wide dirt paths, cleared through forests and fields. "Improvements" generally meant the widening of these roads to accommodate teams of oxen and rare measures to clear and straighten the paths. As late as 1790, one farmer in Norwich, northwest of Mystic, described the road from that town to Providence as "nearly covered with stones, and the road to Providence is so bad as to render the transportation of produce very inconvenient and expensive." In the early nineteenth century, the roads might be raised slightly, with the grade leveled and covered in gravel. Still, at best, when the roads were dry and unfrozen, travelers could expect to cover an average distance of four miles per hour. Thus, aside from the postal service and the stagecoach service, which only utilized the Boston Post Road, most roads served local economies and communities. They connected small farms to local manufacturing, and villages to local waterways that might bring them in contact with trade and communication with the wider world.

THE VILLAGES AND THE ATLANTIC WORLD, 1700–1815

The Mystic River itself was not a major navigable waterway. Extending inland only a few miles, and affected by the saltwater tides, it served only a small geographical area. Instead, the river achieved importance in the role of a harbor or cove, providing protection for waterborne vessels from storms or attack during the nearly constant wars of the eighteenth and early nineteenth centuries. While none of the villages along the banks of the Mystic River grew into anything resembling a port, in combination with the local roads the river provided the citizens of the surrounding towns with access to larger urban areas and allowed them to participate in the coastal trade as mariners, fishermen, merchants and consumers. As a result, the interests of Mystic became entangled with the interests of those in the colonies who wished to promote free maritime trade regardless of its support by the English government.

Throughout both the seventeenth and eighteenth centuries, European powers fought a steady stream of wars against one another over trade, territory and royal succession. Inevitably, the fighting of these wars was not limited to either Europe or to the land. Wars in Europe provided opportunities to seize colonial territory overseas and control coastal and transatlantic shipping routes. Often, the goal was not to take or control a particular territory or sea route, but simply to rob the land and ships of their stores and cargo. The various European governments, England included, sanctioned this form of piracy, called "privateering."

The English colonists, such as those in New London and the Mystic villages, usually expected the English government to serve two functions during these imperial wars. They expected the English navy to protect colonial ships and coastal towns from attack by enemy navies or privateers. They also expected the English government to refrain from passing laws that might restrict or regulate the flow of trade into, out of and among the colonies themselves.

The English government, in turn, expected the colonists to serve the English mercantile goals. The government expected the colonists to ensure that a significant portion of the profits of trade, predominantly with the West Indies, made its way to England itself. This also precluded trade with the merchants of enemy powers, the allies of enemy powers or the colonies of enemy powers, which some New London merchants were known to do. The government also expected the colonists to support English military action either by enlisting in the English military or, more commonly, by supplementing the English military with colonial militia. For much of the eighteenth century, the amicable relationship between the English government and its American colonies relied upon the ability of each to compromise with the demands and expectations of the other.

The villages on the Mystic River again lay at the periphery of much of the action in these eighteenth-century imperial wars. As late as 1773, one of the greatest perceived threats to their community came not from the French or the British, but from smallpox, the dreaded disease of the eighteenth century. Even a single case led to fears of epidemics and patients were quarantined, preferably as far from the surrounding community as possible. In 1773, Dr. John Loomis, Dr. Philip Turner and Daniel Lee opened a smallpox hospital on an island at the mouth of the Mystic River, possibly the one known as Ram or Mystic Island. There they treated patients and experimented with early forms of inoculation. Because inoculation involved actually infecting the patient with the virus, the process was viewed with often-justified suspicion, if not outright hostility. Loomis was arrested and jailed in Norwich only a year later for his experiments. The hospital on the Mystic River island, meanwhile, was burned in outrage by the surrounding population.

Despite this more immediate danger, the proximity of the Mystic villages to the coast affected the inhabitants' participation in European conflicts. To be sure, when called upon to defend New England, Mystic men responded. They were part of an overland expedition to Montreal in 1690 and the Louisbourg expedition of 1745. They also faced the same threats of French naval attacks that plagued the New England coast. At the same time, Mystic men were also vulnerable to English press gangs that seized colonists for involuntary service in the royal navy. While they had benefited from the government-sanctioned privateering that thrived in New London and Newport, they also profited from smuggling and suffered when both were restricted after the Seven Years' War in 1763. In 1763, too, they also became subject to English restrictions upon manufacturing in the colonies and the enforcement of the Navigation Acts and other regulations on colonial trade. While daily life around the Mystic River resembled that of a farming community, its ties to maritime commerce determined its loyalties in the American Revolution once hostilities began.

In 1774, the English government passed the Enforcement Acts, closing the port of Boston and demanding reparations for tea destroyed in protest of the Tea Act. Citizens of both Groton and Stonington met and declared sympathy with the citizens of Boston in direct violation of the Enforcement Acts. They also formed Committees of Correspondence that included prominent members of the communities around Mystic, such as Dudley Woodbridge, Joseph Packer, Charles Eldredge Jr. and members of the Gallup family. The Portersville village on the west bank of the Mystic River was reported to have erected a Liberty Pole as an overt demonstration of their sympathies, and Captain Abel Spicer of the Groton militia led his men to aid the colonists gathered at Bunker Hill. New London also threw in its lot with the colonial rebels.

For the first two years of the Revolutionary War, the British strategy focused on dividing New England, which the English government assumed was the only rebelling region, from the other nine colonies. Much of the fighting took place between Boston and New York. Even after the fighting moved west and then south, the British navy maintained a blockade on Long Island Sound, with ships patrolling out of Manhattan and Narragansett Bay. The patrols were charged with enforcing British navigation laws, apprehending colonial raiders and preventing colonial smuggling. For survival, they often requisitioned colonial crops and livestock. "Requisition" often involved seizure. Near Mystic, farmers who used the strip of land called Groton Long Point as a common grazing ground lost much livestock to British raiders from Newport.

During the war, New London earned a reputation as a center for privateering. New London was a target because of the privateering carried on at that port during the Revolution. Many of the leading New London citizens, including the Shaws and Saltonstalls, had a stake in the enterprise, either as captains, shipbuilders, ship suppliers

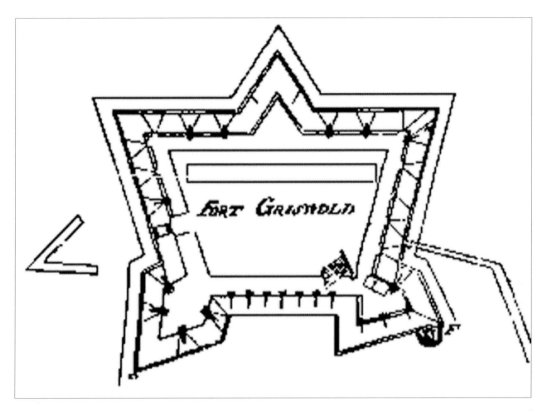

A plan of Fort Griswold, which stood on the Groton side of the Thames River, across from New London. Citizens from Mystic and the surrounding towns gathered here to defend the waterway from a British invasion led by Benedict Arnold in 1781. *Bill Memorial Library, Groton, Connecticut.*

or investors. Less prominent citizens participated as crewmembers. As a result, a steady stream of prizes entered the Thames River throughout the war, carrying rum, flour, sugar, coffee, cloth, candles, tools and other trade goods no longer readily available due to the war. Seamen and fishermen in Stonington Borough, led by the Palmer family, also conducted their own voyages, and anyone with access to a whaleboat led raids on the Tory outposts on Long Island. Indeed, the merchants of New London proved so effective in their privateering that the Continental Congress commissioned them to outfit its first naval expedition in 1776.

All of this activity naturally drew the attention of the British to New London. In 1776 and 1777, British naval vessels anchored in the Thames harbor, and New London remained a target in following years. Stonington Borough also drew fire in August 1776. Already, the colonists had determined a need for fortification along the Thames River and began constructing Fort Griswold on the heights above Groton Bank in 1775, opposite Fort Trumbull in New London, which had been completed the year before. These two forts became the scenes of battle in 1781.

In 1781, the English strategy turned to the Southern colonies. At the same time, hoping to distract General George Washington and divide his forces, the British planned an attack on a Northern target. The consistent privateering out of New

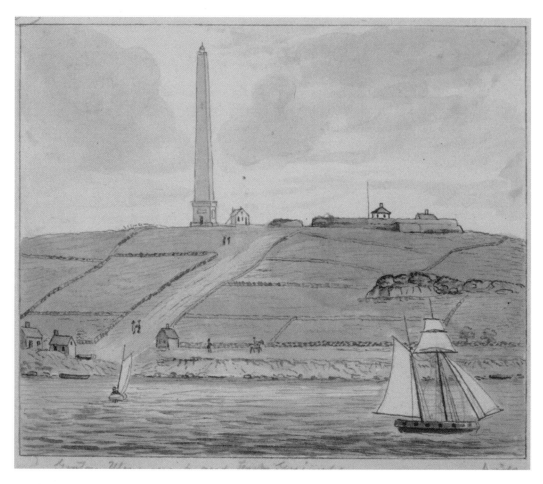

The site of Fort Griswold, including the 1830 monument. *John Warner Barber Collection, Graphics Collection, Connecticut Historical Society.*

London made it the likely choice. General Benedict Arnold, a Connecticut native and former general in the American Continental army, was eager to prove his loyalty to the British and led this expedition. On September 6, his forces landed on both sides of the mouth of the Thames River and advanced northward. Arnold, on the western side, led 400 troops toward New London, defeating the militia at Fort Trumbull and burning the town. Across the river on the Groton side, Major William Montgomery led another 400 soldiers to Fort Griswold, which was defended by 150 militiamen commanded by Colonel William Ledyard. Although Montgomery was killed breaching the walls of the fort, his forces defeated the colonials. Ledyard, too, was killed, supposedly at the moment of surrender. Arnold's force then burned Groton and retreated. This operation effectively ended the privateering out of New London.

The Mystic villages were spared the brunt of these raids and assaults. Nonetheless, villagers participated in all of the actions and gathered supplies for the militia. The river itself provided protection for raiders and smugglers hiding from the British, but the nature of smuggling naturally precluded accurate record keeping that would

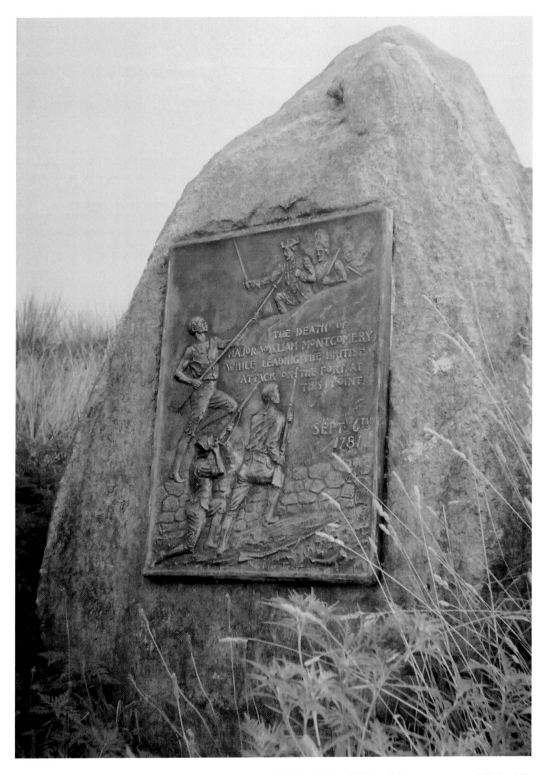

Memorial in Fort Griswold marking the point where British Major William Montgomery was killed while breaching the fort walls. The plaque also depicts one of the African American defenders of the fort. *Photo by author, 2006. Used with permission of Bill Memorial Library.*

determine the extent of involvement by the Mystic villagers. During the war, however, the first signs emerged of Mystic's shipbuilding possibilities.

While the construction of small watercraft, such as whaleboats and other small vessels, probably occurred throughout Mystic's history, the first records of shipbuilding as a business appeared in 1779 and 1784. The constant military activity and market for vessels on the Thames River during the Revolution was likely the stimulus for Daniel and Eldredge Packer to explore opportunities in this arena. Additionally, fishing out of Noank and Stonington Borough had grown, and sealing had begun in earnest. Both of these enterprises had created a demand for vessels that could travel far into the north and south Atlantic or down the coast to Florida.

In the decades between the end of the Revolution and the War of 1812, the Packers continued to build ships, and their shipyard at the lower Mystic River villages was joined by the Enoch Burrows shipyard and the Christopher Leeds shipyard at Head of the River, and the Morrill shipyard farther downriver. Their successes drew other shipbuilders to the area, if only for the construction of a handful of vessels. This emerging industry strengthened the Mystic villages' ties with the maritime economy and gave them a greater stake in the events leading up to the War of 1812.

After the War for Independence, American merchants, such as those in New London, returned to the West Indies trade with great enthusiasm. Unfortunately, continued wars between the French and English through the 1790s and into the 1810s, and attempts on the part of both to force the United States into an alliance, took the place of English regulations. Any act on the part of the United States that could be interpreted as friendly toward one of the belligerent nations was automatically interpreted as an alliance by the other. Additionally, the English continued impressments by boarding American vessels within sight of American shores. Pressed sailors included Mystic resident Jeremiah Holmes, who escaped after three years of forced service. In an attempt to preserve neutrality, the U.S. government passed a series of embargo and non-intercourse acts in 1809 and 1810, cutting off trade with both Britain and France until both or either respected U.S. neutrality. While the French ultimately acquiesced, the English continued to treat the United States as quasi-colonial subjects. In the end, when England and France went to war, the United States joined in against the British in 1812.

As in the American Revolution, the British blockaded Long Island Sound and raided coastal communities; and, as in the American Revolution, the Americans from Newport to New York did their best to break the blockade and conduct their own privateering raids upon the British navy. Mystic, now supplying ships for the surrounding merchants, had moved closer to the center of this action and danger. A battery was erected on Pistol Point for defense of the river, while those on the Portersville side fortified a large outcropping of granite, which they called Fort Rachel.

Most of the military action involving Mystic and the surrounding area took place offshore, as ships attacked and claimed one another as prizes, many as close as Block Island. But in June 1813, a British vessel attacked two American merchant vessels at the mouth of the Mystic River. Led by Captain Jeremiah Haley, twenty men from Mystic were able to drive off the British vessel. A few months later, in October, a British vessel

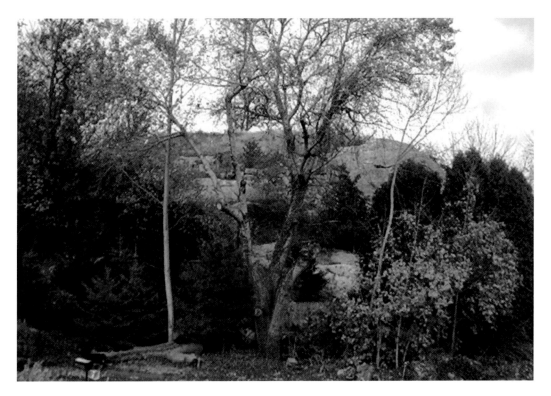

Fort Rachel, little more than a battery, sat at the top of this granite ridge, guarding the approaches to the lower villages of Mystic. Tradition holds that the fort was named for a congenial woman, "Aunt" Rachel Park, who lived in a house below the ledge. *Photo by author, 2006.*

again entered Mystic harbor. The gunmen at Fort Rachel forced it to retreat. The vessel then tried a different approach, sailing around the eastern side of Masons Island. When the tide went out, however, the vessel ran aground in the mud.

The Mystic area found itself embroiled in a larger action just over a year later. In August 1814, the British turned their guns on Stonington. On August 9, four British vessels commanded by Captain Thomas Hardy appeared in Stonington Harbor off Stonington Borough. Hardy ordered the town evacuated and surrendered. Many of the borough residents gathered their belongings and left the town, but the militia stayed, and soon was joined by volunteer forces from Mystic that included Silas E. Burrows; Nathaniel Clift; Jeremiah and Frederick Haley; and Frederick, Ebenezer and Isaac Denison Jr. Jeremiah Holmes, the previously mentioned veteran of British impressments, was also in their number. When the Americans refused to surrender the town, the British began bombardment. For the next two days, both sides exchanged fire. The Americans finally repulsed the British attack on August 11. The residents of Stonington declared a victory, having protected their homes from invasion. The British, however, moved farther down the coast in search of another target.

The next day, at the mouth of the Mystic River, one of the British barges was sent to pursue a fishing sloop captained by Simeon Haley. Haley's small vessel lured the barge close to shore along Groton Long Point. The barge ran aground and was immediately attacked by a militia of forty men led by Captain John Barber. Years later, a British captain was supposed to have called Mystic "a cursed little hornets' nest" for just such operations. After this, Mystic did not suffer any further attacks, and peace was declared at the end of the year.

The end of the war led to a long period of peace for the residents of Mystic, which meant prosperity. With shipbuilding emerging as a reinvigorated business and with the establishment of the Mystic Manufacturing Company, Mystic could no longer be characterized as a peripheral, coastal, farming village. Instead, the Mystic River villages would become a cohesive community of shipbuilding and manufacturing, fully involved in the industrial, transportation and market revolutions of the nineteenth century.

CHAPTER 4

A VILLAGE OF SHIPYARDS, 1815–1914

In the nineteenth century, Mystic entered its most prosperous era, with an economy founded upon shipbuilding, but led by entrepreneurs who knew to diversify their investments and adjust to change. In this century, the dominant businessmen changed from craftsmen to capitalists, exploring the limits of investment possibilities until the changing nature and scale of the maritime economy outgrew the Mystic River Valley and forced them to leave or adapt. Diversification and adaptation led them to manufacturing, which outlasted shipbuilding, but never quite reached the same heights of wealth. Meanwhile, the different builders and proprietors of businesses ancillary to shipbuilding formed partnerships across specialties, creating, in essence, a series of informal interlocking directories. As a result, the Mystic villages came to resemble a company town. Despite straddling the border between two towns and retaining similar but separate names, Mystic became a cohesive community.

By the end of the War of 1812, shipbuilding had already emerged as a growing business along the Mystic River. The Packers, the Leeds and the Burrows were already building ships, and builders from New London and Groton Bank on the Thames River would occasionally appear to use the riverbanks for their own constructions. This pattern continued into the 1820s and was not limited simply to shipbuilders. On Christmas Day in 1816, the sailmaker's apprentice Charles Mallory wandered into town from New London, heading toward Boston to seek his fortune. He, as others after him, saw the possibilities in the maritime trades on the Mystic River, and he stayed to open his own sail loft. The Mystic River—out of the way, unfettered by traffic and as yet undeveloped—provided opportunity for those with the skills and the capital to begin a new venture.

With the exception of Silas Enoch Burrows and Charles Mallory, these earliest shipbuilders were predominantly craftsmen with a focus on producing ships. Some, like the Leeds brothers, operated shipyards in a variety of locations and contracted their labor to other shipyard owners. They also employed some of the later builders and craftsmen who would form the elite of the Mystic capitalists. Burrows would be the first of these capitalist shipbuilders to see the wealth generated by these vessels that he constructed and fit with sails.

If Burrows ever performed much manual labor on the ships that his and his father's yards produced, that portion of his career was quite short. Instead, his area of expertise lay with the business side of shipbuilding and shipping. In the 1820s, he opened a packet line out of New York that ran to South America where, in 1833, he sent two shipbuilders in his employ, Clark and Thomas Greenman, on an unsuccessful attempt to build a river steamer. Burrows, however, seldom stayed in Mystic for long. While he continued to employ Mystic shipbuilders, and built a large mansion on the Groton side of the river, most of his business activity took place in larger venues farther away. He himself circumnavigated the globe, engaging his vessels in the China trade and Pacific whaling, and his main business offices operated out of New York and, after 1851, San Francisco.

Mallory, however, stayed closer to home for a longer period of time and was more typical of the businessmen who prospered in Mystic. Indeed, he, along with his sons, was the epitome of Mystic businessmen. He seemed to have the monopoly on sailmaking in Mystic when, within ten years of his arrival there, he sensed the enormous wealth to be had in whaling. Although that fishery would not begin to expand until the 1830s, with its peak in the 1840s, Mallory began to purchase shares of the early equivalent of "stock" in whaling voyages, receiving a percentage of the profits of the voyage, by 1824. Two years later, he began to do the same with the coastal trade, which would begin bringing in profits from the cotton trade within the next decade, as well as lumber, sugar and rice from the Southern states. When Florida entered the union, interest in the coastal trade led to involvement in the lucrative salvage business off the Keys. Additionally, Mallory began to speculate in the cargo of these voyages and helped his son David form a mercantile partnership with Isaac W. Denison. So busy was Mallory with these other ventures that he did not actually enter shipbuilding until 1851, when he purchased the shipyard of Captain Peter Forsyth on the east side of the river. A few years later, his son, Charles Henry Mallory, purchased a second yard across the river from his father's yard.

By that time, two of the other three important Mystic shipyards had already appeared on the Mystic's banks. The Greenmans—Thomas, George and Clark— opened George Greenman & Co. on Adams Point, a stretch of land protruding into the river about midway down its length, which became the site of Mystic Seaport in the twentieth century. They had each apprenticed with their father Silas, a Westerly shipbuilder. Following their older brother, Silas Jr., they moved to Mystic to work for Silas E. Burrows. Silas Jr. returned to Westerly, but the other three brothers stayed and opened their own yard in 1837. Around 1841, the next shipbuilding firm opened, located on Pistol Point. Dexter Irons, who had launched his own ships during the late 1830s, entered into a partnership with Amos Grinnell. The two had formerly worked for the Leeds. The final major shipyard, Maxson, Fish & Company, would open in 1853 with six owners, several of whom were already successful in other businesses.

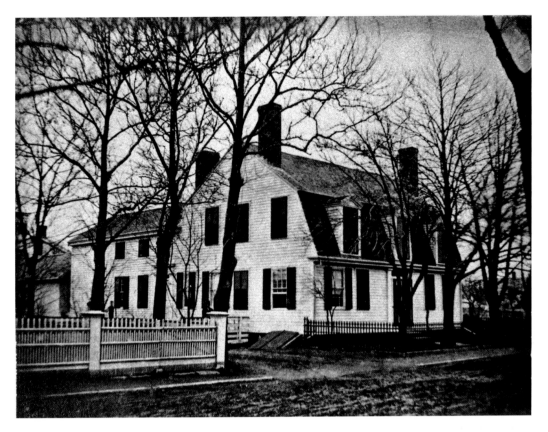

The Asa Fish house, photographed here in the late nineteenth century, was one of the first homes in the lower village that formed on the eastern side of the Mystic River, the area soon to be known as Mystic Bridge. *Mystic Seaport Collection, Mystic, Connecticut, #76.166.5.*

The opening of these yards signified a change in the focus of settlement on the river. The earliest shipyards had been located at Head of the River, where most of the population of Mystic also congregated. These newer shipyards appeared in the deeper water farther south on the river, around the villages of Lower Mystic and Portersville. As the major business of the valley moved to these villages, so did their owners and workers. Thus, while the village at the head of the river retained the name "Mystic," these other two were, in fact, the focus of most of the major activity on the river.

As the various businesses of the town became entwined with the shipbuilding industry, so did their communities. This was further enhanced by the construction of the first bridge across the river. In 1819, a state-chartered stock company built a wooden drawbridge at the narrowest point across the river. The location roughly coincided with the ferry crossing, but not exactly, which meant that the routes of the roads had to be altered. On the Stonington side the bridge passed near enough to Willow Street to prevent any major difficulties. This village, in fact, soon became known as "Mystic Bridge." On the Groton side, however, the road that led all the way from Groton Bank ended at the ferry landing. The bridge lay approximately a quarter of a mile north of the landing. Thus, the route from the road had to make a jog.

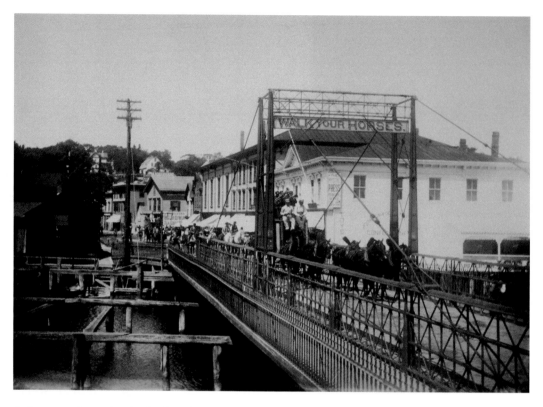

A circus parade crossing the first iron drawbridge from West Main Street in Mystic River to East Main Street in Mystic Bridge. This drawbridge was erected in 1866 to replace the last wooden bridge. *Mystic Seaport Collection, Mystic, Connecticut, #1980.41.712.*

To reach the bridge at Portersville, a traveler from Groton Bank would now pass through the Poquonnock plain, skirt around Fort Hill and among the hills of the granite ridge on the western side of the river. At the bottom of a steep hill, the traveler would make a sharp right onto Water Street, which was often underwater in rainy weather and high tides, and then proceed north around a small inlet from the river, finally making a sharp right turn to the bridge. This road after the last turn, leading directly to the bridge, became West Main Street, and the intersection became Bank Square. The greater integration of these two villages was suggested when the Mystic River Bank was organized in 1851, and Portersville became Mystic River. Now, three villages claimed the appellation "Mystic" in their names.

These two villages on the lower part of the river were both the focus and the major beneficiaries of the capitalist brand of businessmen, as exemplified by Charles Mallory, whose business ventures flourished between the 1830s and the 1870s. This period coincided with the most lucrative years in large fisheries, an exploding textile industry and the demand for fast sailing vessels to skirt Cape Horn. The unregulated nature of nineteenth-century commerce allowed companies to form without permission from government and permitted a variety of business relationships that would result in a maximum profit with a minimum of risk.

The business of doing business during the early nineteenth century was also undergoing a revolution. In the early years of the nation, most businesses required a charter from the state or federal government, and the business owners' personal and professional finances were closely entwined. No longer fettered with government charters, as the company that built the Mystic River bridge had been, and vested with limited liability, the potential emerged for businesses to grow much larger in scale. All of the shipbuilders on the Mystic River had incorporated either in families, in partnerships or, as time passed, in a combination of the two. Additionally, business relationships remained almost wholly unregulated, allowing partnerships to form not only among competitors but also among businesses with overlapping interests.

For New England, whaling and textiles would be the biggest of businesses. Mystic was never one of the major whaling centers, ranking fourteenth or fifteenth in its number of whalers at sea during the most profitable years. Still, whaling investments in Mystic nearly equaled those of shipbuilding during its best decade, 1838 to 1848. In 1845, at the height of Mystic's involvement in whaling, twenty-seven ships in the American whaling fleet hailed from the Mystic River, with Mystic investors owning shares in more. Additionally the third largest business in town was focused on outfitting these vessels for voyages that could last up to five years. Mystic may not have rivaled the whaling capitals of New Bedford or New London, but within the town itself, whaling enjoyed a period of great importance.

At the same time, the textile industry drove both the New England and the national economies during the same years and beyond. Mills proliferated in towns along the major rivers, such as Norwich on the Thames River, fed by the explosion in cotton production in the South. Shippers could reap great profit by transporting cotton crops to factories in both New England and Britain, then returning with the manufactured cloth, and this was only a part of the shipping fortunes that could be made on the coast and across the Atlantic.

In an attempt to expand and diversify their own investments, the Greenman brothers went in the direction of textiles themselves by opening the Greenman Manufacturing Company next to their shipyard. They generally produced woolen manufactures rather than cotton, following the example of John Hyde, whose Mystic Manufacturing Company had been operating at Head of the River since 1818. The Greenmans' decision to focus on woolen goods also may have been driven by the availability of wool closer to home. John Brown, that most radical of abolitionists, pioneered this method of profiting from the textile industry while refusing to support slave-grown cotton.

Cotton and textiles were only a fraction of the shipping fortunes that could be made in the nineteenth century, particularly after China opened to foreign trade in the 1840s and Americans began to rush to California for gold and land. These two developments attracted such investors as Burrows and Mallory and, more importantly for Mystic, led to a demand for ever-faster sailing vessels. In 1853, the Irons & Grinnell yard produced one of the more famous of these clippers, the *Andrew Jackson*, which rivaled the *Flying Cloud* in speed around Cape Horn, and the Greenman brothers launched the *David Crockett*, which produced over $300,000 in profit for its various owners over the following twenty years. Even when not producing the bigger, faster sailing vessels, the

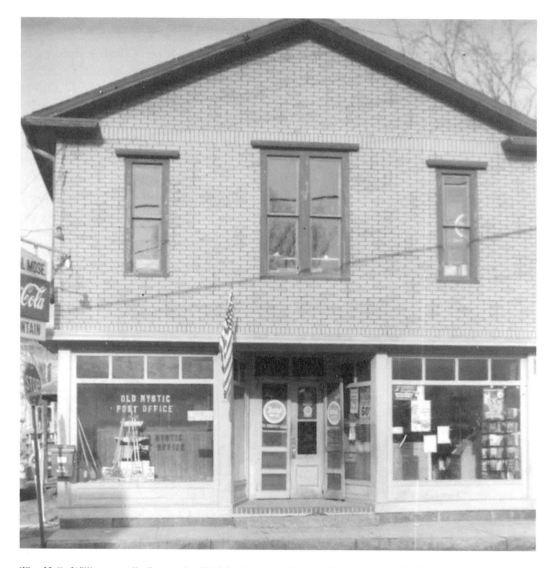

The H.O. Williams textile factory in Old Mystic, much like the Greenman family factory farther south, ran a company store for its employees where the workers could receive credit or exchange company script for necessities. *Photo from Indian and Colonial Research Center, Inc., Old Mystic, Connecticut.*

Mystic shipyards maintained a steady stream of packet ships, coasting schooners and brigs and fishing vessels of all sizes.

While the shipbuilders expanded their wealth by servicing and investing in these global industries, in Mystic their success translated into a boom for the rest of the town. The shipyards themselves required labor, both skilled and unskilled, as employees and contractors. All of the ancillary businesses and industries that supported or stemmed from shipbuilding had these same needs. Young men from Mystic, other coastal towns and the surrounding countryside flocked to the river, eager to work or become apprentices. During the Civil War, when shipbuilding had reached its height,

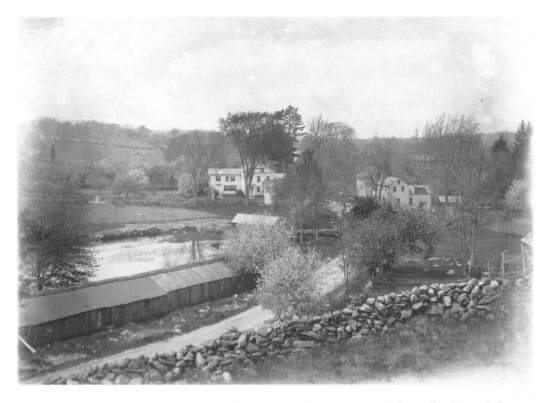

While shipbuilding was the largest industry in Mystic, other businesses, such as the line walk at Burnett's Corners (Old Mystic) shown in the lower left corner of this picture, developed around the Mystic River to supply fish and net line for local and regional use. *Photo from Indian and Colonial Research Center, Inc., Old Mystic, Connecticut.*

the population around Mystic nearly doubled. Thus, while Mystic remained culturally homogenous, it avoided much of the xenophobia, racial, cultural and labor conflicts that plagued urban areas such as Boston and New York.

Certain skills, however, provided the craftsmen with the opportunity to open their own business. In so small a community, many businesses ancillary to the shipbuilding industry could establish monopolies. Charles Beebe & Son ran the one ropewalk that supplied the Mystic shipbuilders, locating his factory at the top of the hill overlooking the Mallory and Greenman yards. The ship carving partnership of James Campbell and John N. Colby served all of the shipbuilders on the Mystic River. John, William and Oliver Batty ran the J&W Batty spar yard, which supplied masts, booms and yards to the shipyards along the river. They also produced blocks and dead eyes, spool-shaped pulley devices, possibly driving the short-lived rival block-making partnership of Johnson & Denison out of business. This company changed hands several times, surviving into 1913, when its last owner died. Blacksmith Lyman Dudley was among the most fortunate. He not only served the smith needs of the shipyards, making all the various ironwork such as chain plates and other accoutrement, but also met the demands of the entire town in an age of horses, buggies and metal farm implements.

Like Dudley, skilled artisans or businessmen who could meet the needs of both the shipbuilders and the surrounding population did very well and, perhaps, had greater security over time due to their ability to adapt much more quickly to change. Lumber, in particular, was a constant necessity for the construction of ships and the buildings that served as homes and offices. After 1820, Joseph Cottrell cornered the lumber market for the ship and spar yards, first with the Cottrell Lumber Company and then, after 1850, with Cottrell, Gallup & Company. As the only lumber supplier on the Mystic River, he also would have supplied the materials for Amos Clift II, who built many of the homes in Mystic Bridge; Lathrop & Northrup, which manufactured window sashes and blinds; and Gilbert Morgan & Company, which built furniture. As with many of the other successful businessmen connected to shipbuilding, Cottrell also invested in the surrounding industries.

As the Industrial Revolution advanced, machinery businesses also became wise investments. Beginning in 1848, Jedediah Randall's Reliance Machine Company produced marine engines, cotton gins, boilers, tools, coffee grinders and other home and agricultural machinery that was sold around the country. In 1847, Isaac D. Holmes approached industrialization from a different angle, opening a business importing and selling coal to power the steam engines, which was increasingly essential in homes, factories and steamships.

The scale of shipbuilding, however, tended to prevent monopolies, and the shipbuilders more frequently experimented with vertical integration techniques perfected by Andrew Carnegie much later in the nineteenth century. In such an arrangement, the owners of the shipyard would also own one or more of the ancillary businesses in order to profit from its use by other builders and to reduce the costs from that particular sector for themselves. Charles Mallory began with his monopoly on sailmaking in his first years on the Mystic River. When he expanded into shipbuilding, he maintained the enterprise, briefly going into partnership first with William N. Grant and then with Isaac D. Clift. Ostensibly independent of the Charles Mallory & Sons shipbuilding firm, the Mallory sail loft continued to supply the other shipbuilders of the river and keep the cost of sails down for his own yard. The Mallory sail loft faced competition from only two other sailmakers: J. & W.P. Randall and Beebe & King.

The Greenman brothers pursued a different route with vertical integration by creating a company town. The economic center of Greenmanville revolved around their shipyard and woolen mill operations. The stately homes of the three Greenman brothers sat in a row along the road that ran parallel to the river, intersecting with Willow Street to the south and running northward to Head of the River. Their houses were flanked by the homes of their skilled employees and the boardinghouses of their mill and shipyard operatives. Amid the dwellings, the Greenmans ran a store that accepted the company script that they issued as pay. Finally, being the only Seventh-Day Adventists in a town largely made up of Congregationalists, Methodists and Baptists, the brothers constructed their own church.

Many Mystic businessmen gravitated toward cooperative ventures. They invested in one another's operations regularly, most commonly in stores that would supply vessels

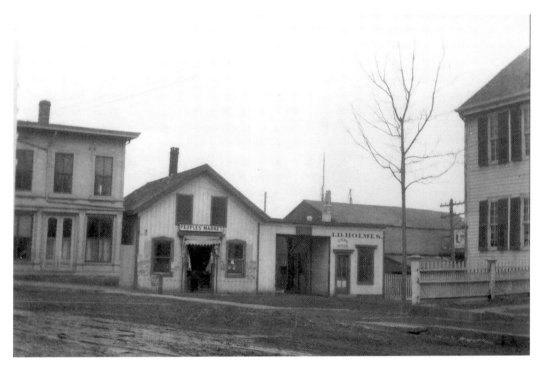

Ships, factories and homes began to rely on coal power, creating a market for the Holmes Coal Company. The company office is shown here at the corner of Holmes and East Main Street. *Photo from Indian and Colonial Research Center, Inc., Old Mystic, Connecticut.*

and sell cargos. Charles Mallory started his son David in a partnership with Isaac W. Denison to open the general store David D. Mallory & Company. Additionally, the elder Mallory owned shares in Ira H. Clift's store, while also maintaining a partnership with a store owned by Cottrell and Benjamin F. Hoxie. Hoxie himself was an investor in various vessels and voyages, and in 1853, he branched into yet another shipbuilding company as one of the proprietors of Maxson, Fish & Company. The Maxson, Fish firm itself was a cooperative effort of several Mystic businessmen, consisting of Hoxie, Captain Nathan G. Fish, Captain William Clift, Isaac D. Clift, William E. Maxson and Simeon Fish.

A more sophisticated form of cooperation in which the men engaged, however, was banking. Prior to the Civil War, joint ventures of the prominent men of Mystic produced three banks. The first appeared in 1833 at Head of the River. Patrons of this bank included Mallory, the Greenmans, Cottrell, Jedediah Randall and all of their attendant companies. In 1851, many of these patrons in turn founded the Mystic River Bank. Along with Mallory—who became the first president—the Greenmans and Cottrell, the board of directors of the Mystic River Bank also included Charles H. and David Mallory, Hoxie, Simeon Fish and Captain George W. Ashby. George W. Ashby and Henry B. Noyes were involved in both banks, and in 1855, they helped to establish Groton Savings Bank of Mystic. Other founders of this third bank included the very same men who had been depositors in the Mystic Bank and founders of the Mystic River Bank. These institutions, including the Mystic Bridge National Bank,

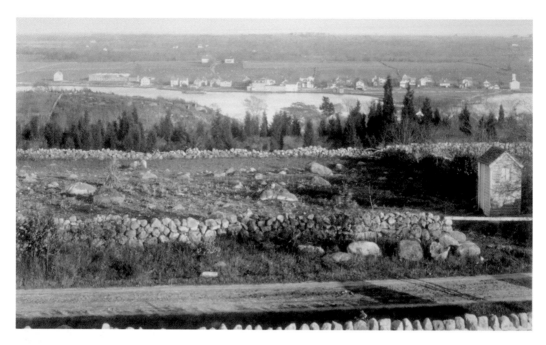

Greenmanville was something of a company town that developed around the Greenman shipyard and woolen factory. The Greenman brothers owned boardinghouses, a store and two farms, and were instrumental in establishing a Seventh-Day Adventists church. The Greenmanville area became the site of Mystic Seaport Museum in the twentieth century. *Mystic Seaport Collection, Mystic, Connecticut, #1970.160.2118.*

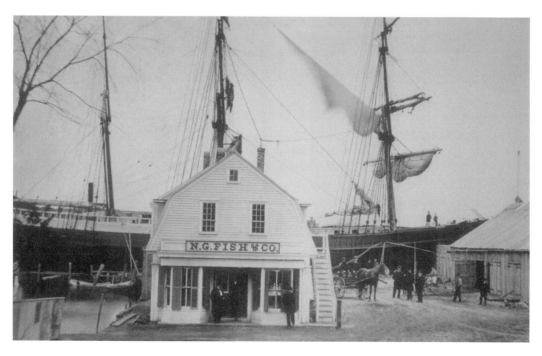

Maxson, Fish & Company, circa 1866, owned by Nathan G. Fish. *Mystic Seaport Collection, Mystic, Connecticut, #1972.882.11.*

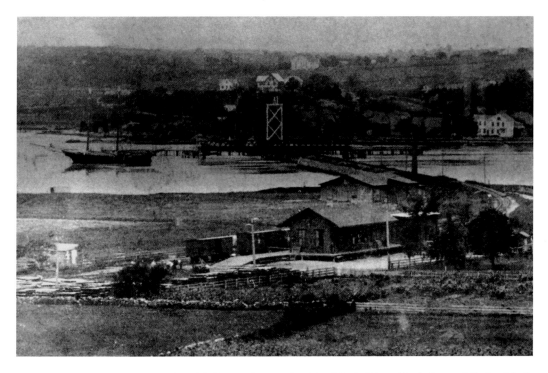

A sailing vessel approaches the railroad bridge at the mouth of the Mystic River. *Mystic Seaport Collection, Mystic, Connecticut, #1993.17.503.*

benefited their founders and the surrounding community by extending credit beyond that available in ordinary business transactions, thereby providing access to funds that would allow even the subsistence farmers who lived in the surrounding towns to expand their businesses beyond their ordinary capabilities. All three of these banks remained local until well into the twentieth century.

Surprisingly, the railroad played little part in much of the rise of industry in Mystic, perhaps because the rail came so late to the villages. Indeed, its delay may have contributed to the success of maritime activity, particularly shipping, in the Mystic area. By some fluke of planning, the coastal line that would connect New York to Boston would not reach the Mystic River until 1858. Nonetheless, many disgruntled victims of the post–Civil War bust in the shipbuilding industry blamed the railroad.

The Civil War marked the greatest boom for shipbuilding, and perhaps for any other business in Mystic's history. The Mystic villages remained removed from the sectional crises of the 1850s. Politically, the voters in the town tended to favor the faltering Whig Party for its dedication to national and industrial development. Also, some support appeared for the Free Soil Party for its opposition to expanding slavery, and a group of citizens sent a petition to Congress supporting the abolition of slavery in Washington, D.C., and opposing any measures to extend slavery.

In general, the population of Mystic was morally opposed to slavery, but was not exceptionally active in the antislavery movement, which was considered

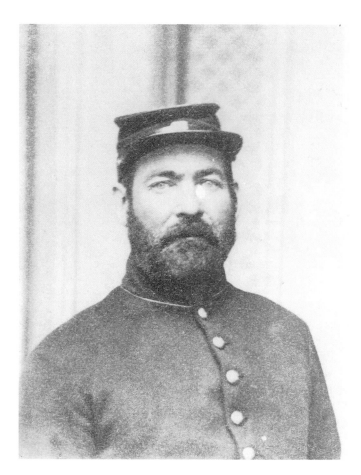

George Waite, grandfather of Old Mystic photographer Elmer Waite, was a soldier in the Union army during the Civil War. Mystic men fought in most major battles of the Civil War, particularly in the eastern theaters of operation, as well as at Port Hudson in Louisiana. *Photo from Indian and Colonial Research Center, Inc., Old Mystic, Connecticut.*

radical even by New England standards. Moral opposition also did not necessarily transform into an economic critique of the system. Such people as Jedediah Randall, who manufactured cotton gins, and anyone invested in the coastal and international cotton trade, even the Greenmans with their woolen mill, had ties to slaveholding states.

When the war came, however, the people of Mystic wholeheartedly supported the Union. Volunteer units formed, drilling and parading through the streets of the villages. Crowds gathered in churches for services dedicated to soldiers and at the train depots to see the men off. Men from Mystic composed parts of the Eighth, Twelfth, Twenty-first and Twenty-sixth Connecticut Infantry Regiments and the First Connecticut Cavalry. These units saw action at Gettysburg, Port Hudson, Antietam and Drury's Bluff. At the last part of the Peninsular Campaign in Virginia, the Mystic men were supported by another Mystic warrior, the ironclad *Galena*. Back at home, those who could not volunteer raised money to support the soldiers, hoping to receive $100,000 in contributions to outfit the men at the front. Patriotism ran high, and in 1862, citizens in Mystic River raised a 120-foot Liberty Pole, memorializing a connection between the war that created the United States and the war that would preserve it.

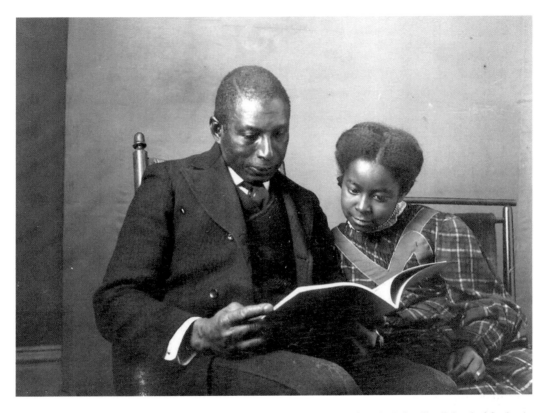

Joseph Bateman and his daughter, Arlee, were members of one of the few black families living in Mystic. As this photograph shows, African Americans were not barred from education in Connecticut. *Photo from Indian and Colonial Research Center, Inc., Old Mystic, Connecticut.*

For the shipbuilders, conversion to the wartime economy occurred quickly and dramatically. Mallory set the pace. First, he liquidated his remaining whaling investments and abandoned the coastal cotton trade, realizing that for the duration of the war trade south of Philadelphia was risky to the point of being unfeasible. He then focused his shipbuilding efforts on steamships. Steam-powered vessels had emerged from Mystic shipyards before the war, but now would become the more profitable types of ships produced there during the war.

The conversion to steamships in turn prompted the Reliance Machine Company to abandon its cotton gin manufacturing. The company now concentrated on marine steam engines. Unfortunately, the loss of the Southern market, along with the debt owed to them by their Southern customers, forced the company into liquidation. Joseph Cottrell and David Mallory also opened a new engine and boiler manufacturing concern, called the Mystic Iron Works, on Pistol Point. This business produced the only iron-hulled vessel from Mystic commissioned for private owners, who were from New York but wanted to use the vessel in Cuba. Otherwise, they built and maintained steam engines and boilers for a year or two after the war's end. But the war's end caused all of their lucrative government orders to stop. This in turn led to the conversion of their large wood mill into woolen manufacturing.

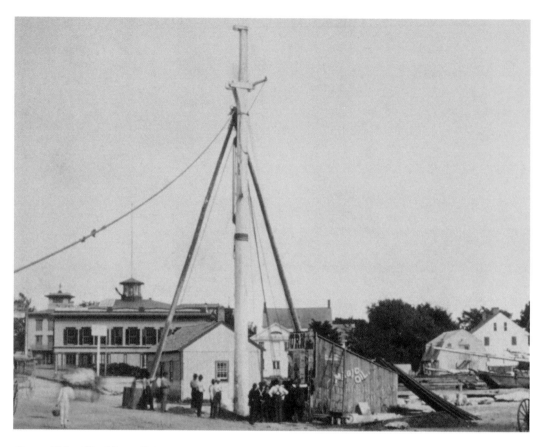

Above and below: The Liberty Pole was originally erected on the west side of the Mystic Bridge in 1862 in response to the war fever generated in the early months of the Civil War. In 1876, it was dismantled, as shown here, and moved to the east side of the river near East Main and Cottrell Streets, but was moved again in 1887 to the intersection of Holmes and East Main Streets, as seen in the second view. *Mystic Seaport Collection, Mystic, Connecticut, #1977.92.671 and #1975.294.413.*

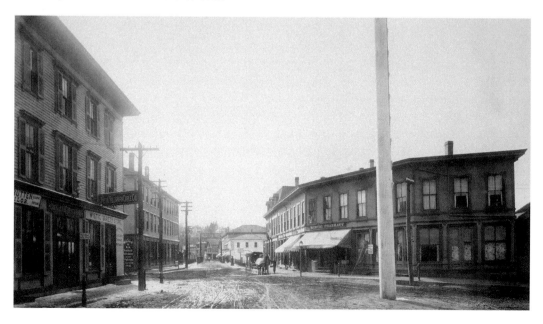

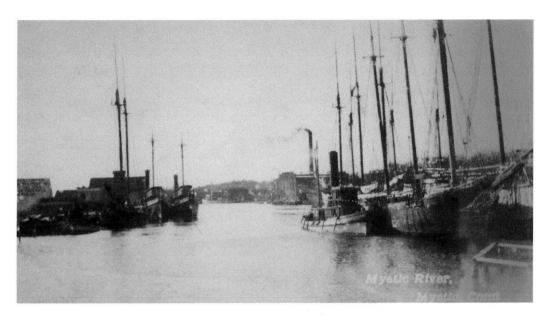

Early twentieth-century shipping activity on the Mystic River included both wooden schooners and steam-powered vessels. *Mystic Seaport Collection, Mystic, Connecticut, #1994.18.39.*

Hill & Grinnell was perhaps the only shipyard that did not benefit much during the war. Formerly the shipyard of Irons & Grinnell, the death of Dexter Irons in 1858 forced a reorganization, in which Amos Grinnell purchased Irons's portion of the shipyard and then entered into partnership with Mason Crary Hill in 1860. Both Grinnell and Hill took positions as naval inspectors during the Civil War and abandoned their business until near the end of the war; but they were the exceptions.

As a whole, Mystic shipbuilders doubled production during the war, increasing their output from eight new vessels per year in the decade before the war to a high of twenty-three new vessels in 1864. Steamship production alone averaged fourteen vessels per year. These included the ironclad *Galena*, built by Maxson & Fish for the navy. Just as the growth of the shipbuilding industry had led to the growth of all businesses in the Mystic villages, so did the acceleration during the war. The lumber and construction business, along with the mercantile business, boomed in accommodating both shipbuilding and immigrants attracted to jobs in the Mystic area.

Yet even as the population grew, factories and shipyards faced labor shortages as most of the able-bodied men enlisted. The war claimed much of the manpower that would normally fill the labor force during peacetime. When the draft was instituted in 1863, businesses in Mystic faced the loss of their most experienced and skilled workers. Charles Mallory found himself driven to sustain his workforce, offering over $800 each to release his most prized employees from service. Release could normally be purchased for $300.

The end of the war was met with much jubilation, even as the villages mourned the assassination of President Abraham Lincoln. In 1864, citizens of the villages had formed a Union Club to support his reelection. Only five months later, over one thousand people gathered in the Union Baptist Church at the top of Main Street in

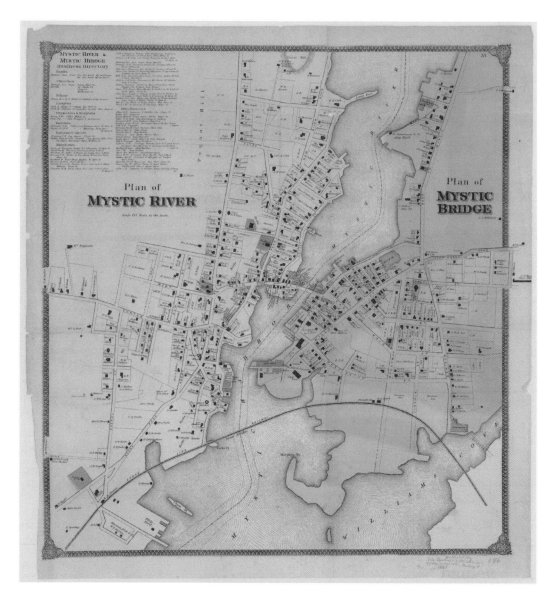

An 1868 map of Mystic, then called Mystic River and Mystic Bridge, showing the villages at the peak of their nineteenth-century development. *Mystic Seaport Collection, Mystic, Connecticut, #G3784.M92 1868.B3.*

Mystic River to hear a service in his memory. The three Greenman houses were draped in black. On the Fourth of July, spirits had recovered enough for a victory celebration that included a parade and a concert by the Mystic Cornet Band.

The end of the war also signaled the end of Mystic's great days of shipbuilding. The cessation of hostilities with the Confederate states had again opened the cotton and coastal markets, but too much else had changed. The whaling investments that had for a time rivaled shipbuilding had also disappeared. The creature itself was badly depleted by overfishing and petroleum had largely replaced whale oil in lighting and lubrication, causing investment in the whaling industry to be less appealing.

Just as the earliest shipyards at Head of the River had been replaced by yards in deeper water farther downriver, these newer shipyards were replaced by others in deeper rivers elsewhere. Even if the Mystic River had been able to handle these larger ships, the center for wooden shipbuilding had shifted to Maine, closer to the sources of lumber and cheaper labor, while the center for iron shipbuilding had moved west to the Delaware River, nearer the mines and mills of Pennsylvania. Mystic businessmen had few options in the face of these forces. They could leave the area, adapt to the limitation of both the market and the geography or change their investing patterns.

Charles Mallory chose the first option. Nearing his seventieth year, he relied more and more upon his sons, Charles H. and George W., to run the business. The shipyard in Mystic Bridge launched its last vessel in 1878. A year earlier, the doors had closed on the sail loft that had remained active since 1817. The yard across the river had closed before the war and was sold in 1866. That same year, Charles Henry Mallory refocused his business on his steam packet lines to New Orleans and Galveston, opening an office in New York that was in partnership with Mystic Captain Eliju Spicer. From then on, C.H. Mallory & Co. was no longer a Mystic concern.

In 1869, Mallory did send business back to his father's shipyard. The Spanish government had contracted with Delameter Ironworks in New York to build thirty gunboats for use against rebels in the Spanish colony of Cuba. Cornelius Delameter had for many years supplied the Mallorys with marine engines, and he asked Charles H. Mallory to build twenty of these boats. Mallory, in turn, offered subcontracts on two to the Greenman brothers and five to Hill & Grinnell.

At the time, American popular opinion was against the Spanish in their efforts to crush the Cuban insurgents, while the federal government had no wish to alienate the Spanish empire. Then the Peruvian government protested. Relations between Peru and Spain grew strained, and the Peruvian government believed that the gunboats would, if not be directly used in an attack on Peru, then at least free other, larger ships for that purpose. In September 1869, as heated negotiations ensued and the boats neared completion, the federal government ordered that the vessels not be released to the Spanish. U.S. revenue cutters patrolled both the New York and Mystic harbors to enforce this order. By the end of the year, the matter was settled with little fanfare. Spain, with the backing of the U.S. government, had assured the Peruvian government that it would not attack. The boats were delivered to the Spanish ambassadors and sent to Cuba, with accounts settled in New York and Mystic. Within a decade, the shipyards of both the Greenmans and Hill & Grinnell would shut down, and by the end of the century, the proprietors would all have passed on.

A series of optimistic entrepreneurs attempted to open shipyards in the early decades of the twentieth century. The Holmes Shipbuilding Company, M.B. MacDonald & Sons, the Gilbert Transportation Company and the Pendleton Brothers were each welcomed with much hope, to the point of great financial investment by many of the Mystic citizens. They all specialized in three- and four-masted schooners, and were all located in the deeper water below the Mystic River drawbridge. Unfortunately, they each closed after approximately three years of business.

You are cordially invited to attend the launching of Schooner

Quinebaug

at the shipyard of M. B. MacDonald & Sons
Tuesday, November 24th, 1903, at 12.30 o'clock
Mystic, Connecticut

Kindly reply
Please present this card upon going aboard vessel

The MacDonald shipyard issued this invitation, inviting the holder to board the schooner *Quinebaug* at its launching ceremony. In 1903, the date of this invitation, such launchings had become infrequent, as shipbuilding had declined on the Mystic River. *Photo from Indian and Colonial Research Center, Inc., Old Mystic, Connecticut.*

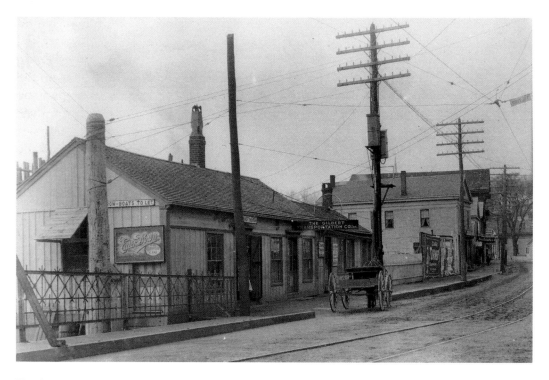

The Gilbert Transportation Company, located on West Main Street, on the southwest side of the Mystic Bridge. This photograph shows the prevalence of telephones and the trolley track, modern innovations in the early twentieth century. *Photo from Indian and Colonial Research Center, Inc., Old Mystic, Connecticut.*

While the younger Mallorys adapted to the postwar depression by leaving Mystic or focusing on other business enterprises, others found that they could survive only by adapting to the changing demands for wooden vessels. In 1876, when Mason Crary Hill reopened his own shipyard on the former site of Hill & Grinnell, he specialized in small steamers for menhaden fishing and small excursion steamers popular with the year-round residents and "summer people" alike. David O. Richmond, who had once worked for Mallory as a ship carpenter and foreman, specialized in the construction of yachts, small fishing craft and small work boats of every variety after the Civil War. His close ties with Charles H. Mallory, a member of the New York Yacht Club, as well as "summer people" in search of leisurely pursuits, sustained his shipbuilding and repair business until his death in 1908. The last shipyard to open in Mystic picked up where Richmond left off. The Franklin Post yard opened in 1914, constructing yachts and small fishing vessels. Post had the good fortune of being open in time to construct liberty boats for the U.S. Coast Guard in World War I, but returned to the yacht and fishing business afterward. The yard, under different ownership after 1959, remained open through the rest of the century.

The grand century of shipbuilding in Mystic had come to an end by the close of World War I. The focus of regional shipbuilding and its attendant maritime industries had moved west to the Thames River. There, in 1900, the Eastern Shipbuilding Company opened and began producing large freighters. Shortly thereafter, in 1911, the New York Ship & Engine Company opened to build submarine engines in World War I. After several reorganizations and mergers, this company would become the Electric Boat Company, or EB. The U.S. Coast Guard established a station on Avery Point in 1911, as well, and the U.S. Navy, which had occupied a yard farther up the river since the Civil War, began to expand. Meanwhile, the economy of the Mystic River altered. Businessmen who had not left, died or changed the scale of their operations now focused on manufacturing and the appeal of the river as a summer resort. As the shipbuilding industry died out, manufacturing for a time achieved the greater importance.

CHAPTER 5

A VILLAGE OF FACTORIES, 1815–1940

All the while that shipbuilding rose and declined as Mystic's driving economic force, manufacturing followed at a slower, less exciting, but more enduring pace. While many of the industrial businesses in Mystic were inextricably linked to shipbuilding, many more operated independently from shipbuilding. These factories provided a consistent supplement to the Mystic economy through the nineteenth and early twentieth centuries as the Industrial Revolution transformed the nation. Yet even these operations passed into obscurity as larger, regional or national corporations swallowed the small, local businesses, until the double blow of the Great Depression and World War II ended small manufacturing.

Because the dominant business in Mystic was shipbuilding, and interest in that aspect of the economy has dominated the study of the region, little attention has been paid to this other aspect of Mystic's economic history. Thus, industrialization in Mystic has been scantily documented. Still, remaining records make clear that, from the earliest grist, saw and fulling mills, manufacturing had been part of life in the Mystic River Valley. Mystic manufacturers have produced a wide and diverse array of items throughout the history of the region. The two most successful categories included textiles and machinery, but in the mid-nineteenth century Mystic entrepreneurs opened a variety of factories to serve the needs of daily life and farming. Mystic's natural resources would also prove ripe for industries, but many of these would come from outside of the area, and those outside influences would serve to save the economy of Mystic while taking much of the management and control over its business away from the region.

The first textile factories in New England appeared in the late eighteenth century, in response to the boycotts and blockades of the American Revolution. In Connecticut, the first woolen mill opened in Hartford in 1788, and the first cotton mill opened in Manchester in 1794. Continued embargoes on foreign trade after the Revolution assisted American manufacturing, but the end of the War of 1812 and the first protective tariffs, as well as the advent of steam power and the creation of corporations to raise the capital to build factories, transformed this early industry into a big business.

In Mystic, the earliest appearance of the textile industry appeared with the fulling mills of the colonial and Revolutionary eras, but in 1807, James Dean opened the first full-fledged factory, followed by James Hyde in 1813. Hyde had owned a variety of mills around Head of the River in the early nineteenth century, which places him among the early Mystic capitalists who saw opportunity as investors rather than craftsmen. His Mystic Manufacturing Company produced woolen goods at Head of the River until 1870. Hyde's factory was joined in Old Mystic by the Taylor Woolen Mill, the Greenman Manufacturing Company farther down the river in 1849, the Oceanic Woolen Company in 1865 and the Mystic Woolen Company in 1866.

The reduction and eventual closure of the Mystic shipyards, which had a ripple effect throughout the rest of Mystic's economy, had left the villages in a depression. Some shipbuilders, in fact, diversified their investments by turning to textile manufacturing. Shipping magnates Charles H. and David Mallory, the Mystic Iron Works firm partially owned by David Mallory and shipyard owner Charles Grinnell banded together to open the Mystic Woolen Company. David Mallory, in fact, held stock in several of the woolen mills on the Mystic River, as well as the nearby Lantern Hill Silex operation. Still, the textile mills clearly felt the downturn in Mystic fortunes when the Mystic Manufacturing Company founded by Hyde closed; the Greenman Manufacturing Company turned to partnerships with businessmen in surrounding states to continue operation; and the Mystic Industrial Company formed to bring both the Rossie Velvet Mill and the Ninigret Silk Mill to Mystic.

The survival of the Greenman mill and the arrival of the Rossie Velvet Mill in 1898 anticipated the future of manufacturing as a whole in Mystic in the twentieth century. Between 1871 and 1897, a succession of owners from Rhode Island and Massachusetts, who were sometimes in partnership with the Greenmans, ran the Greenman Manufacturing Company. In 1897, the English company of H.A. Crowther purchased the mill and renamed it the Mystic Manufacturing Company. These owners kept the looms running until U.S. government inspectors enforced regulations that eventually led to the closing of the mill after 1924.

The same year that the Greenman mill passed into foreign hands, a cooperative of Mystic businessmen banded together to form the Mystic Industrial Corporation. The corporation, in an effort to benefit Mystic by skirting the high 1890 tariffs on imports, invited German velvet manufacturers Ernest, John and Thomas Rossie to open a mill in Greenmanville. Thus, two of the largest factories in Mystic were not locally owned. Yet this need for greater amounts of capital, which could only be found outside of the area, was necessary for the economic survival of Mystic.

Textile manufacturing had appeared early in Mystic and was, for the most part, separate from the shipbuilding business. The manufacturing of steam engines and boilers began later and was more closely tied to shipbuilding. The earliest machinery company was the Reliance Machine Company, which actually served both the textile and the shipbuilding industries. Appearing in Mystic in 1848, the factory churned out cotton gins, although it periodically provided Mallory & Sons with steam engines. At

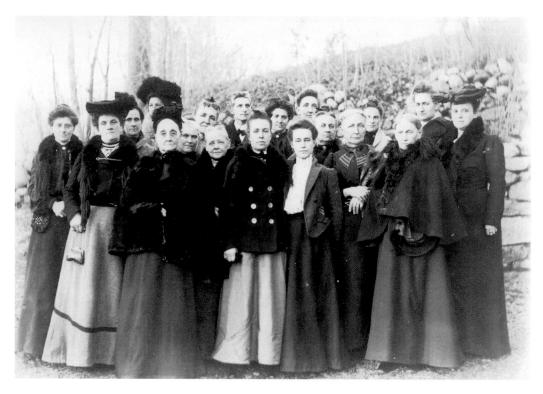

As in other textile factories throughout New England, women formed a large part of the workforce in Mystic. Women were prominent among the laborers at the Greenman woolen mills, the Rossie Velvet factory and other mills throughout Mystic. *Photo from Indian and Colonial Research Center, Inc., Old Mystic, Connecticut.*

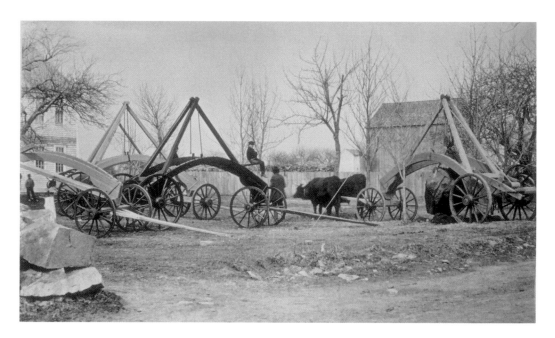

Although agriculture was not a major part of the Mystic economy, the rocky soil continued to plague farmers and construction workers. Here, workers demonstrate a rock and stump puller developed and patented by entrepreneur George Washington Packer in 1865. *Mystic Seaport Collection, Mystic, Connecticut, #1972.882.1.*

the start of the Civil War, Reliance converted entirely to marine engines and boilers, but the loss of both the Southern market and the debts owed by Southern customers doomed the company by 1862.

By that time, Mystic Iron Works, owned by David Mallory and Joseph Cottrell, stepped in to fill the gap left by Reliance. In opening this company, Mallory and Cottrell had hoped to be the first shipyard on the Mystic River to construct iron-hulled ships. Such production did not prove feasible after the construction of just one, the *Montaines*, in 1863, and the factory concentrated on steam engines and repair work instead. As the textile industry also used steam power, Mystic Iron Works could meet the needs of that business as well, and found its salvation in that direction after the war. In 1866, its factory, which had shared a building with the Oceanic Woolen Company, became part of the Mystic Woolen Company as David Mallory and his associates adapted to the postwar depression in shipbuilding.

Marine engines continued to be the most common type of machinery manufacturing in Mystic during the late nineteenth and early twentieth centuries. Most of these engines, however, were designed for small vessels, due to the increasing popularity of yachting and the ongoing need for fishing boats. In 1897, J.W. Lathrop & Company replaced Mystic Iron Works as the main manufacturer of marine engines. James Lathrop had already dabbled in textiles with his twine factory and also ran a witch hazel distillery, both located in the Burnett's Corners section of Groton. J.W. Lathrop & Company, later the Lathrop Engine Company, was joined by other small outfits such as the Hasbrouck Motor Company, the West Mystic "Autoboat" Motor Company and the Broughton Company. Most of these companies were single proprietorships and seldom outlived their owners. Only the Lathrop Engine Company survived World War I; it did not close until 1954.

The mid-nineteenth century, from 1845 to 1890, saw a flurry of small manufacturing in Mystic, little of it associated with either textiles or shipbuilding. Most ordinary people in the area around Mystic continued farming, leading to the development of businesses geared toward their needs. One of the earliest was Charles Johnson's carriage- and wagon-making shop, later called Johnson & Denison, which opened in 1844. In 1848, G.W. Packer & Co., later Packer & Fish, began the production of an odd device that would pry boulders and stumps from the ground. In 1866, the Mystic River Hardware Manufacturing Company began selling agricultural tools. Much of the fishing along the coast produced not only food, but also fertilizer useful in specialty crops like Connecticut River tobacco and other agricultural uses throughout the nation. This was produced by numerous menhaden fishing companies in the Mystic area, including the G.S. Allyn & Company fish works on Masons Island and Leander Wilcox & Co. on Latimore Point, which were two of the largest.

Mystic manufacturers also met the needs of households, not only through construction of homes, but also in furnishing appliances and daily necessities. Most homes were built from lumber that passed through the Cottrell & Gallup Planing Mill. Lathrop & Northrup provided sashes and blinds in 1848, and Cottrell & Company took over that market in 1866. The Gilbert Morgan Company made furniture beginning in 1849, and the households of Mystic could acquire folding dolls' beds and cradles from C.A. Fenner & Company in 1873, then from I.D. Clift & Company a decade later. By 1887 they could purchase a Eureka rolling chair. Meanwhile, E. & L. Watrous manufactured such daily appliances as clothes wringers beginning in 1870. Fenner & Company also manufactured toys, and children of Mystic could play games or locate Mystic on a globe made by the Cheney Globe Company beginning in 1889. If anyone at home fell ill, then housewives could administer the cure-all, witch hazel, from one of the distilleries in nearby Poquonnock Bridge or Burnett's Corners, or from the Mystic Distilling Company, founded in 1896.

Packer's Tar Soap proved the most successful of these factories serving the household market. In fact, the rise of this business serves as an example of how many entrepreneurs transformed their businesses from cottage industries to full-fledged factories. In 1870, Captain Daniel Packer began cooking tar soap in his own kitchen. Gradually, he was able to hire female assistants. As the popularity of his soap grew, production moved to a larger building on the Groton side of the river, and then to a factory next to the railroad depot on the Stonington side in 1906. The company remained in Mystic until 1967.

Some factories completely defied categorization. One of the most adaptable of these was the Standard Machine Company, with roots in the mid-nineteenth century as the Reliance Machine Company and reborn after liquidation as the Sanborn Machine Company, which manufactured bookbinding machinery and paper cutting machines, but later shifted to plastic moulds. Another was the Allen Spool & Printing Company, which opened in 1888 to manufacture spools for thread and printing blocks. With the exception of the Standard Machine Company, however, most of these small factories did not survive into the twentieth century.

The final industrialized business that would bolster Mystic's economy during the decline of the shipbuilding industry was not specifically a manufacturing business. Beginning in 1860, when the Markham Rock Quarry opened to extract rock for paving the streets of New York City, the granite outcroppings around the Mystic River became attractive to other such companies. Near the turn of the century, E.S. Belden & Son opened a quarry on Masons Island to create the breakwater at Saybrook and elsewhere in southern New England. Porter's Rocks fell to the Russell Welles Company in 1871 in order to pave the streets of Norwich. Similarly, the silex or silica of Lantern Hill became the target for mining, with David Mallory among its leading investors. Silica enjoyed a brief popularity into the early twentieth century; but, as with the granite quarries, the mine closed down later in the twentieth century.

In the 1920s, the new character of the Mystic economy was becoming apparent. By that time, shipbuilding, along with the large-scale manufacturing required of the larger vessels, had moved west to the Thames River, where the Eastern Shipbuilding Company and the New York Ship & Engine Company had opened just before World War I. The war itself had given a slight boost to the Post shipyard and to the Lathrop Engine Company, which received government contracts for the U.S. Coast Guard.

For the most part, however, by the close of World War I, Mystic had become a summer resort town and most of the businesses in Mystic were retail outlets that served the surrounding community through the Variety Store, Rexall Drugs, local

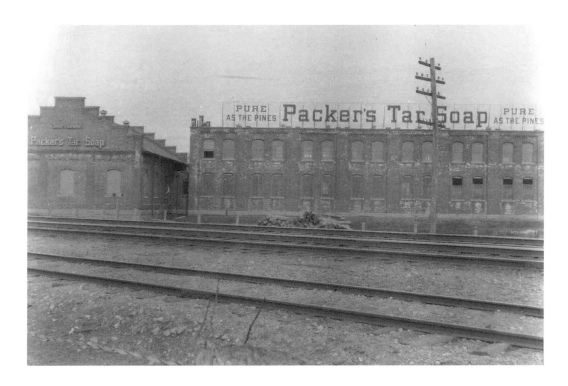

Above: The Packer Tar Soap Company was one example of the manufacturing that replaced shipbuilding as the focus of Mystic's economy after the Civil War. *Photo from Indian and Colonial Research Center, Inc., Old Mystic, Connecticut.*

Right: Hattie Crandall, wife of Louis Crandall, was a cook at the Packer Soap Factory. Her husband worked as a dyer at the Rossie Velvet Mill. *Photo from Indian and Colonial Research Center, Inc., Old Mystic, Connecticut.*

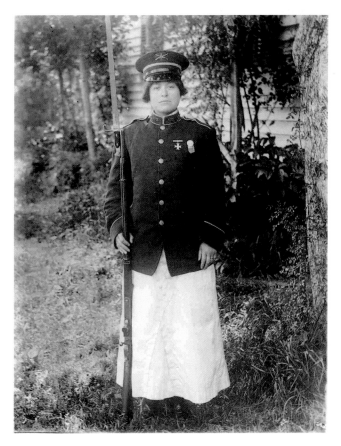

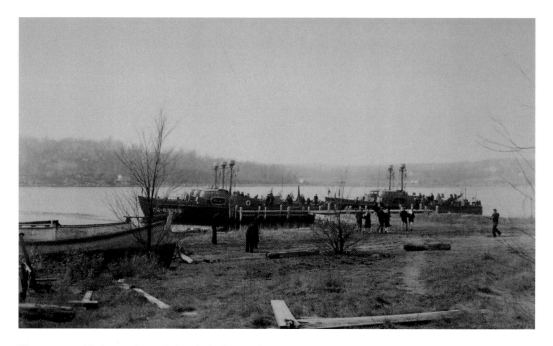

The war provided a much-needed revival of manufacturing in Mystic that produced the material for soldiers' uniforms, marine engines and small boats for the military. Here, five coast guard patrol boats, powered by Lathrop engines, dock on the Mystic River prior to being turned over to the government. *Mystic Seaport Collection, Mystic, Connecticut, #1983.70.27.*

bakeries, laundries, clothing stores and groceries. The transportation revolution that Mystic experienced with the advent of trolleys, automobiles and the creation of U.S. Route 1, which incorporated Main Street and the New London Road, facilitated and fed this retail economy. Louis Doyle opened a garage as early as 1906 to repair the vehicles passing through, and in 1920, Sebastian, Joe and Aldo Santin opened the first auto dealership on Greenmanville Avenue. They later went their separate ways, with Aldo "Bud" Santin opening a dealership on Roosevelt Avenue (part of Route 1) and Joe starting his dealership on Holmes Street, just north of the bridge, to also take advantage of the traffic from Route 1.

The Great Depression ended any potential for economic growth for a decade. Those factories that survived only did so through massive reorganization. The Sunoco Corporation of South Carolina purchased the Climax Tube Company, a later incarnation of the Allen Spool Company. The executive sent to manage the Mystic branch was G.W. Blunt White, an avid yachter, who not only gave a boost to the Post shipyard, but also became a local philanthropist.

The Rossie Velvet Mill faced greater trouble. During World War I, because the Rossies were German nationals, the mill property was seized under the Alien Property Custodian Commission. Their American agent, William Openhym, purchased the factory at auction and business once more resumed. During the Depression, repeated cutbacks in production, hours and wages led the workers to form the National Association of Velvet Workers union. Conditions continued to deteriorate until, in

1936, the union went on strike. The strike was quickly settled, but the workers' union joined the Congress of Industrial Organizations (CIO) the following year. Conditions did not improve for anyone involved in the mill, however, and the company closed twice. The first closing took place in 1937, when Openhym declared bankruptcy. This allowed the Rossie family to purchase and reopen the mill. Two years later, the mill closed again. This time, the William Johl thread factory, which had shared the same building since before the war, also closed, suggesting that conditions in Mystic had grown worse. The two were able to consolidate their businesses and finally reopen on a smaller scale in 1940.

The year 1938 proved to be the most disastrous of all for Mystic. On September 21, one of the largest hurricanes to reach New England shores slammed across Long Island and into the Connecticut coast. The storm measured approximately five hundred miles in diameter, with a fifty-mile-wide eye that passed between Saybrook and Westerly. The submarine base at Groton reported a barometer reading of 28.62 and anemometer reading of ninety miles per hour before its equipment blew away. The storm was followed by a surge, made worse by the high tide, that most residents remembered as a "tidal wave."

Mystic was overcome. Boats were lifted out of their moorings and set down onto the railroad track, across streets and wedged between homes. The railway station collapsed. Centuries-old trees that had survived deforestation were uprooted, leaving holes the size of caves. Whole roofs flew off homes and buildings. Bricks fell from downtown stores, with whole loads dumped onto the streets below. Bank Square flooded, along with all businesses and homes between it and the river. Telephone poles blew down and fires broke out. The building housing the Standard Masons Island Yacht Club was entirely destroyed. The Methodist church on Willow Street imploded into splinters. The Union Baptist Church at the top of West Main Street was decapitated when its landmark white steeple blew off. Throughout New England, the hurricane caused upward of $300 million in damages. Coastal towns such as Mystic easily suffered losses of $1 million. In 1938, recovery was not easy, nor would repairs be complete for nearly a decade. The church steeple would not be replaced until 1969.

Between the eight years of depression and the crippling hurricane, no new industries or businesses would emerge in Mystic until World War II. At best, companies like Packer's Tar Soap maintained production without going into bankruptcy. The Standard Machine Company had done the same until the hurricane badly damaged its factory. All companies experienced cuts in wages. In 1937, however, relief began to appear. That year, the Durham Enders Company of New Jersey opened a factory making aircraft engines and torpedo parts. After surviving the hurricane, Durham Enders would become one of the two wartime industries to open in Mystic. The other, Connecticut Cabinet Company, opened in 1941 and received contracts for the U.S. Signal Corp. The final factory to appear in Mystic would be the Sirtex Printing Company, which arrived in 1942. The company took up residence in the Mystic Manufacturing Company mill in Old Mystic, where it printed fabric designs.

During World War II the majority of industrial activity continued and grew on the Thames River. Production at the EB submarine yard drew workers desperate for employment, while the navy's submarine base brought in sailors and their families. As a result, the population of the town of Groton doubled from roughly eleven thousand people in 1940 to approximately twenty-two thousand in 1950. Housing could barely keep pace, even with assistance from the Federal Emergency Housing Project, which built the community of Fort Hill Homes off Route 1 in Poquonnock Bridge. Once again, Mystic became the shopping center for this influx of people.

Once the war had ended and the industries on the Thames River had settled into Cold War production, nine factories were left standing in Mystic. All but two would disappear within the next twenty years. The first to go was the Rossie Velvet Mill and its partner, Johl and Company, which closed not long after the war. The Standard Machine Company was bought in 1952 by the Davis-Standard Company, and switched from manufacturing molded plastic to extruding machines. Ten years later, Crompton-Knowles took over and moved the factory to nearby Stonington. In 1953, Sunoco Products left Mystic. After 1954, the Lathrop Engine Company passed through a series of different owners until 1964, when its latest owner, the Burmiester & Wain American Corporation, closed it altogether. The Durham Enders Company turned to manufacturing razors after the war, and then sold its factory to the Weck Corporation in the early 1950s. Weck manufactured surgical knives until closing in 1979. In 1963, the Connecticut Cabinet Company moved to Norwich. The Packer Soap factory moved to New Jersey after it was sold to Cooper Laboratories in 1967. Sirtex survived in Old Mystic into the 1990s. Mystic manufacturing had been taken over by larger, national corporations, which then moved the factories away from town. Subsequent manufacturing would not originate from the Mystic community, but instead would consist of branches of national corporations.

Industrialization permitted scales of production that outstripped the natural and capital resources of Mystic. As a result, the people of Mystic were forced to look to outside investors or industries to revive or supplement their own businesses or to provide jobs. While this tactic saved many of Mystic's larger factories, it ultimately led to the exodus of most industries. Instead, Mystic was finding itself to be part of a regional economy rather than a center unto itself. By this time, the village had begun to capitalize on its attraction as a summer resort and as a retail center and suburb for industries in Groton.

CHAPTER 6

A RESORT COMMUNITY IN A
PROGRESSIVE AGE, 1870–1940

By the end of the nineteenth century, a new population appeared in Mystic. Arriving as the months grew warm, they disappeared shortly thereafter. These were the "summer people," summer vacationers and artists attracted to Mystic for its scenic beauty and quiet atmosphere. They represented a new industry, emerging as both shipbuilding and manufacturing declined in Mystic. Yet tourism was only emerging as a new part of the economy that instead relied upon retail shops supporting the surrounding community. Meanwhile, the permanent residents self-consciously devoted themselves to developing a year-round community by forming civic organizations to reform and improve the village. Modernization in the form of public utilities, telegraph and telephones, trolleys and improved roads helped to facilitate both of these transformations.

Another name change for the villages during this time signified the greater sense of community, as well as a shift in its geographical center. Before 1890, the three villages along the Mystic River went by three different names. The village commonly called "Head of the River" was the only one known as simply "Mystic." The village on the eastern side of the river was called "Mystic Bridge," and the village on the western bank went by "Mystic River." In 1890, the U.S. Post Office designated these lower villages collectively as "Mystic," indicating as much their interdependence socially and economically—despite being politically and geographically divided between the towns of Stonington and Groton—as outsiders' perception of them as a single entity. The village Head of the River took the name "Old Mystic." Thirty years later, the shift in names continued to displease some, or as Charles Q. Eldredge wrote in his 1920s memoir, the name change "made much feeling, some of it which exists today." Still, the distinctive character and unity of the villages, particularly those around the bridge, had been noted, so much so, in fact, that by 1913 the Mystic Men's Club proposed that Mystic be incorporated as a town separate from both Groton and Stonington. They eventually abandoned this plan.

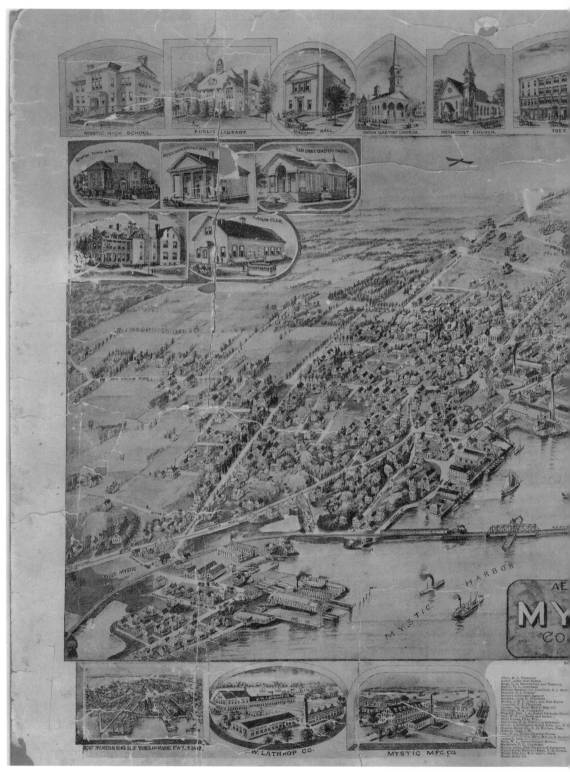

By the time of this 1911 bird's-eye view, the lower villages of Mystic Bridge and Mystic River had become known collectively as Mystic, while the village formerly known as Mystic or "Head of the River" was called Old Mystic. *Mystic Seaport Collection, Mystic, Connecticut, #G3784.M9A3 1912.82.*

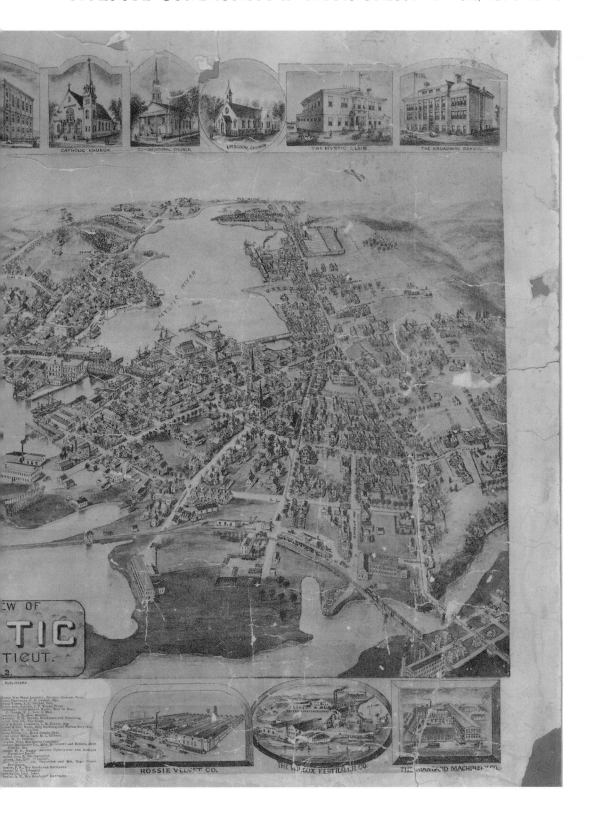

Prior to the alteration of names, outsiders, such as the vacationers who became ever more prevalent as the nineteenth century progressed, seemed to believe that the name Mystic referred to the lower if not all three villages, and this assumption may have also prompted the name change. These outsiders, called "summer people" as an indication of their temporary residence, would have a profound impact upon Mystic for over a century more.

As early as the 1850s, Americans began to embark upon summer trips to resorts in the mountains or on the coast for extended periods of relaxation. At first, only the rich could engage in this activity because only the rich could afford the time and cost of transportation and lodging for vacations. After the Civil War, particularly in the 1870s, more Americans began to go on vacations or tour the country in greater numbers. The railroad had increased the speed of travel while lowering the cost, and more Americans were able to spend a number of leisurely days escaping the crowded pollution of urbanized areas for the health benefits of rural environments.

Mystic had always had travelers, but they had only passed through Mystic, stopping for a night at taverns such as that run by Dudley Woodbridge, then moving on. This pattern continued into the nineteenth century, even after Mystic's two hotels replaced the taverns. In 1818, Nathaniel Clift had built the U.S. Hotel on the southeast corner of the intersection of East Main and Holmes Streets, near the drawbridge. Lodging accommodations occupied the second and third floors, while various businesses occupied the street level, including, at different times, a barbershop, a Western Union Telegraph Office and a drugstore. The U.S. Hotel burned down in 1858, only to be replaced by the Hoxie House hotel, owned by Benjamin F. Hoxie, in 1861. The Hoxie House remained in business into the twenty-first century, suffering several fires and a second name change. It primarily served either people who rented rooms for long periods of time or travelers, and was not specifically designed for the vacationers who sought more than simple room and board accommodations.

In 1850, the second Mystic hotel opened, although it was actually not located in Mystic itself. Instead, visitors to this hotel took a steamboat from Willow Point in Mystic River to Ram's Island, also called by the more romantic-sounding name of Mystic Island, at the mouth of the Mystic River. The hotel there was part of a resort, where visitors could play croquet, bowl, fish, sail or sit on the beach. By the 1880s, visitors could also take short excursions to other resorts in the area, such as the ones developing on Bushy Point and Avery Point in Groton, and Watch Hill in Rhode Island. This vacation destination remained open until 1921, when declining attendance during World War I forced the resort to close and the building was torn down.

In the post–Civil War years, Mystic's attraction as a vacation spot received its greatest boost from the Universal Peace Union's annual meeting each August. The Universal Peace Union had been founded in Providence in 1866 by a group of reformers whose belief in nonviolence after years of bloody warfare led them to a broad critique of American imperialism, U.S. immigration and Native American policies. The local branch had formed among the Rogerene Quakers around Ledyard, and the first national meetings took place in private homes there. As the

A RESORT COMMUNITY IN A PROGRESSIVE AGE, 1870–1940

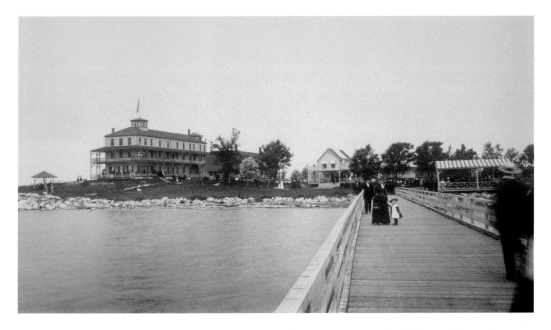

Mystic Island, also known as Ram's Island, at the mouth of the river, was the site of a large nineteenth-century resort hotel called the Nauyaug House, and later, as shown here, the Mystic Island Hotel. Visitors from New York and Boston were ferried to the resort from Noank and Mystic, and at one time enjoyed a private beach, bowling and, in 1870, the bare-knuckle boxing championship fight between Billy Edwards and Sam Collyer. *Mystic Seaport Collection, Mystic, Connecticut, 1977.92.33.*

number of members grew, including large numbers of women, the annual meeting moved to a larger venue in Mystic.

By the 1880s and 1890s, the gathering attracted as many as ten thousand attendees. In 1890, the organization purchased land from Silas Burrows and the Fish family on a hill overlooking the river on the northwestern side of town. Meetings then took place at this open and undeveloped spot, attracting such speakers as reformer Lucretia Mott and author of "The Battle Hymn of the Republic" Julia Ward Howe. Attendees swelled the hotels, boardinghouses and private homes where owners rented out rooms for the occasion. Vendors set up wagons to sell lunches and souvenirs. The rest of town proved so clogged with the traffic from pedestrians and wagons heading to the meeting that those who could not profit from the visitors closed down for the duration of the event.

With so many people, the gathering sometimes turned into a raucous affair. Diarist Helen May Clarke, age thirteen, reported her grandmother's memory of the meetings, writing, "It stared out well enough, but there was soon drinking and it became like a circus or fair." Indeed, the combination of high spirits, alcohol and freethinkers led to more scandalous behavior. "I once heard her speak of a 'Peace Meeting baby,' so I guess there must have been plenty of excitement." Clarke continued, "It would be pretty embarrassing and inconvenient to have a baby at a meeting."

Peace meetings reached the height of their popularity in the mid-1890s, but fell almost completely out of favor during the Spanish-American War. Membership in the union dropped and attendance decreased until the union held its final summer

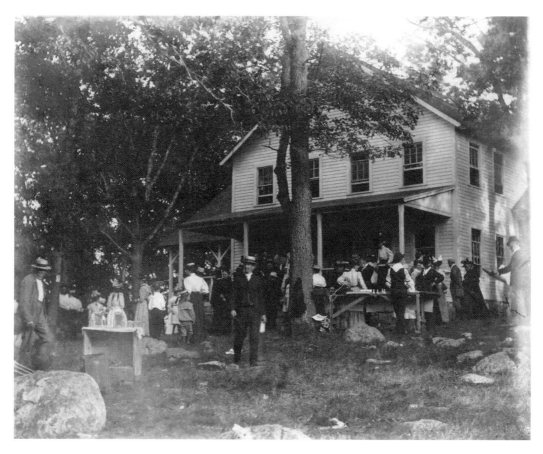

From the end of the Civil War until the beginning of the Spanish-American War, thousands of people descended upon Mystic to attend the August peace meetings. As the size of the meetings grew, the peace society built a pavilion, but most meetings were conducted outdoors when weather permitted. *Photo from Indian and Colonial Research Center, Inc., Old Mystic, Connecticut.*

meeting in 1906. Ten years later, the union sold the property to Mary L. Jobe, the wife of African explorer Carl Ackley, who turned the site into a summer girls' camp.

The peak years of the Universal Peace Union had coincided with the rise of Mystic as a vacation destination, and its status as such lasted long after the union had dissolved. Many resorts at that time found themselves host to the annual meetings of national professional and reform organizations. Many of the attendees then stayed on for a few days to enjoy the resort. Mystic was no different. The annual meetings brought in visitors who found Mystic not only a lovely place for a peaceful retreat, but also much more affordable than the larger resorts at Newport, Saratoga and Long Branch, New Jersey. Thus, peace meeting participants would stay a bit longer and recommend the location to their friends back in New York and Boston.

While the peace meeting drew many visitors for more than three decades, the greater and more enduring attraction of Mystic was its location on the seacoast. Cities in the industrial age of the late nineteenth century were crowded and filthy, with pollution clogging the streets, air and water supply. As early at the 1850s, those

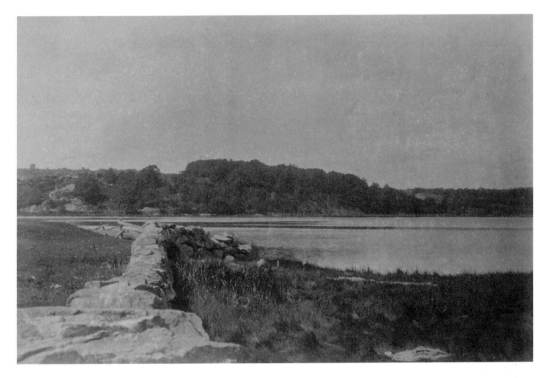

Burrows Grove, partially located on a hill on the western side of the river, served as the summer meeting site for the Universal Peace Union. Later, the site became a girls' camp run by Mary L. Jobe, and later still, it became a nature preserve known as the Peace Sanctuary. *Mystic Seaport Collection, Mystic, Connecticut, #1980.26.3.*

who could escape to healthier environs did, particularly in the summer months. At the same time, many people were feeling the regret expressed by Frederick Jackson Turner, who had pronounced the frontier closed after analyzing the 1890 census. Americans romanticized this passing agrarian age and its rugged way of life. Camping became a recreation that connected them to a hardier past, while providing the benefits of fresh air, fresh food and physical activity.

By 1880, campers had begun to appear on Masons Island, which was largely uninhabited and was occupied only by a menhaden processing plant until 1883. The first of these campers pitched tents, fished, hunted and otherwise "roughed it." Soon, temporary structures appeared in the form of tents with wooden bases, which were subsequently replaced by summer cottages by 1895. The Nauyaug Yacht Club appeared on the island in 1914 and served as a community center for the summer residents for the few years that it remained open before World War I.

The girls' camp run by Mary L. Jobe on the old peace meeting site was part of this increased interest in camping and influx of summer visitors to the area. The girls who attended her camp all hailed from well-to-do urban families in search of a healthy summer diversion for their daughters. Jobe's camp had the added benefit of providing not only outdoor physical activities, such as boating, horseback riding and swimming, but also lectures given by imminent scholars in a variety of fields. The camp was so

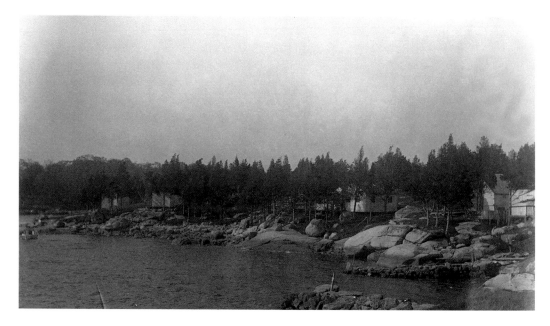

Masons Island, at one time owned by John Mason and his descendants, was largely undeveloped until the end of the nineteenth century, when it became a popular picnic and summer campsite, as seen in this picture. During Prohibition, the island also served as a hideout for rumrunners. *Mystic Seaport Collection, Mystic, Connecticut, #1985.94.72.*

successful that Jobe purchased Mystic Island, after the resort there had closed down in 1921. The girls then took excursions to the island for picnics. The stock market crash, however, drastically reduced the number of visitors to the camp, and the camp closed down in 1930.

Mystic also began to attract artists in the early twentieth century. The countryside around Mystic remained ripe for land- and seascapes. Even the distinctly working-class nature of the banks of the river, particularly below the drawbridge, appealed to visitors. Twelve-year-old Helen May Clarke described the aesthetic appeal of Mystic when she wrote in her diary of the summer visitors that she encountered, "saying how quaint everything was." These visitors even found the muddy and impoverished "Bogue Town" on Water Street "very quaint" because "of course they do have local color as the artists say."

Clarke was writing in 1919, by which time southeastern Connecticut had developed a small but significant art colony. Beginning in 1899, a group of American impressionists began gathering in Lyme, twenty-four miles to the west of Mystic, under the patronage of Florence Griswold. This colony grew quickly, staging its first art show in 1902 and forming the Lyme Art Association in 1914, which would eventually open the Lyme Art Gallery in 1921.

The first artist to make a significant impact upon Mystic was Charles H. Davis. Davis was noted for his impressionistic landscapes, winning first prize at the National Academy of Design in 1917. In 1890, he had taken up residence in Mystic, and after World War I, he became the center of a group of New York artists who joined him at his home on Masons Island each summer. In the following decades, they began building homes near Davis's and farther down the western bank of the river, in Noank. By the 1930s, these artists included Garrett Price, known for his *New Yorker* magazine covers and comics, and marine artist Yngve Soderberg, as well as Carl Lawless, J. Eliot Enneking and Henry Ward Ranger.

Mystic also boasted its own artists, the most prominent of whom was photographer George Tingley. Tingley had learned his craft from one of the early itinerant photographers in southern New England, Everett A. Scholfield. Scholfield had operated a studio in Mystic as early as 1865, and eventually opened branch studios in New London and Putnam, Connecticut. Tingley began working for Scholfield in 1884 and became his photographic partner from 1886 to 1894, and soon began to distinguish himself as an artist outside of his community. In 1898, the Photographers' Association awarded Tingley the silver medal for photography and the bronze medal for portraits at their annual competition. In 1903, his two photographs, "Edge of the Wood" and "Light Beyond," received gold medals from the Photographic Society in Moscow, Russia, and positive comments from such photographic notables as Peter Henry Emerson.

In addition to Tingley and Scholfield, two other amateur photographers worked in Mystic during the late nineteenth and early twentieth centuries. Elmer Waite, son of a Civil War veteran, photographed his neighbors and various sites in and around his home of Burnett's Corners, near Old Mystic. Julia Coates did the same in Mystic. Both photographed portraits, landscapes, interiors and life studies. All four photographers, and many others—including Addison Scholfield (Everett's brother), David O. Angell and Tingley's protégé, Edward Newbury—represented the local contribution to this new art form and left some of the earliest photographic records of the Mystic region.

The Mystic art scene was not limited to famous or professional artists. Beginning in 1914, local artists banded together for exhibits in the Broadway School. In 1926, participants in these exhibits formed the Society of Mystic Artists. Four years later, the society changed its name to the Mystic Art Association and began raising funds to build a facility for its own gallery.

By World War I, a slight change in the attractions of Mystic had occurred. Camping remained popular, but during the 1920s, some of the more popular camping spots, such as Masons Island, were developed as summer homes. The peace meetings were gone, as was the Mystic Island resort. Instead, a new form of entertainment was rising in the form of the casino. Casinos in these early years were not centers for gambling, although perhaps some form of that pastime did take place around casinos. These early casinos resembled what later generations would call nightclubs. Dancing to live music provided the main attraction, and advertisements for casinos always boasted the quality of the dance floor. As a 1927 ad for the Wequetequock casino promised, fifty cents would gain admission to "the same old place with a Reputation for Good Music, a Good Floor, a Good Crowd, and a Good Time." Two decades earlier, the Wequetequock casino, which had opened in 1906, was also the first place near Mystic to show a motion picture. The club opened every summer until 1940, when it burned

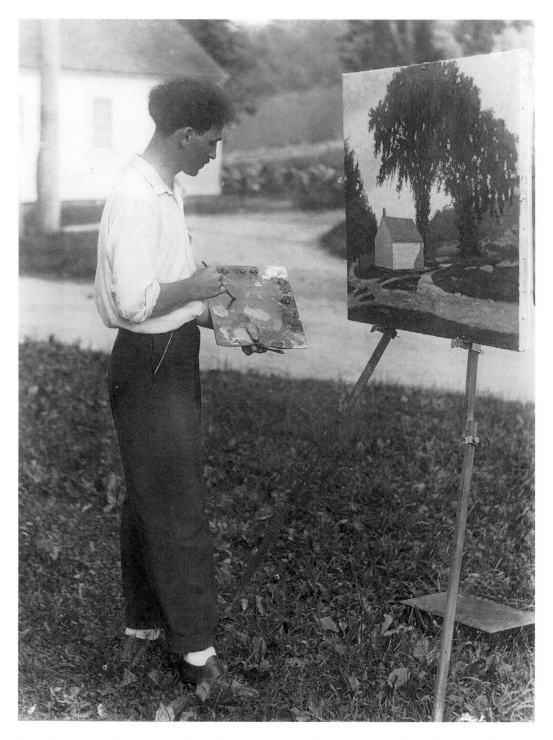

In the late nineteenth century, southern Connecticut attracted many artists. Although the center of artistic activity was at Lyme, Connecticut, to the west, the Mystic River and its surroundings also served as the subject for many American impressionists, such as local artist Ben Green, shown here, as well as nationally known artists such as Henry Ward Ranger and Colin Campbell Cooper. *Photo from Indian and Colonial Research Center, Inc., Old Mystic, Connecticut.*

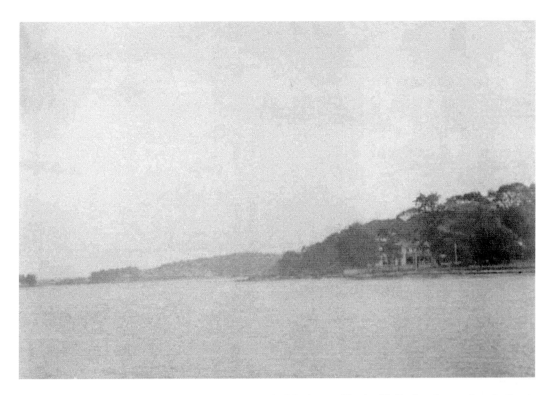

One of the most famous artists to spend his summers in Mystic was Charles H. Davis, who purchased a home on this site. He persuaded many of his friends from the New York art world to join him. Local artists also proliferated, and together they formed the Society of Mystic Artists, later to become the Mystic Art Association, in 1925. *Photo from Indian and Colonial Research Center, Inc., Old Mystic, Connecticut.*

down. In addition to the Wequetequock casino, on the road between the Mystic River and Pawcatuck, Mystic also entertained another casino on Willow Point, just below Fort Rachel. The Willow Point casino, which opened in 1915, used the old West Mystic Boat Company's building for a dance hall.

While liquor was still legal, these casinos served alcohol. The combination of liquor and dancing made casinos all the more popular with young people. During World War I, Helen May Clarke, who lived on Fort Rachel, described some of the "goings-on" of the casinos when liquor combined with dancing. A French ship had docked nearby, and the sailors all crowded into the Willow Point casino, where they became so rowdy, so frequently, that Clarke "had to take my hammock down because soldiers and sailors with their girls were using it at nights."

Officially, casinos and the "two or three" (by Clarke's count) local saloons abided by the Prohibition laws once they were enacted. How strictly Prohibition was observed, however, cannot be determined. Rumrunning, or the smuggling of alcohol, was commonly known to be a constant problem in Long Island Sound. In fact, the Post shipyard in Mystic turned out small powerboats that earned the name "rumrunners" because they were often used in just such activity. Rumrunners were often apprehended in waters near the Mystic River. In 1928, one vessel was apprehended off Stonington.

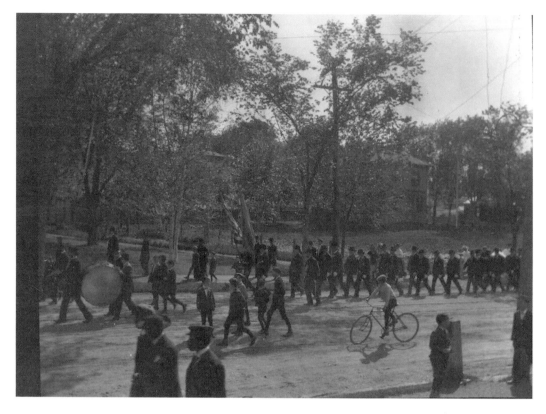

In 1919, young diarist Helen May Clarke wrote, "Most of my friends had someone in the war." Young men from the area, seen here marching in a Memorial Day parade, joined the armed forces and Home Guard during World War I. *Photos from Indian and Colonial Research Center, Inc., Old Mystic, Connecticut.*

The same year, Joseph Radicioni and Benjamin Coneau were convicted of "keeping of liquor for sale and for keeping a house with a reputation."

Yachting, too, became a popular activity for summer residents after World War I. The first yacht club in Mystic, the Nauyaug Yacht Club, opened on Masons Island in 1914. That same year, the Post shipyard in Mystic began to construct their rumrunning vessels. Although the Nauyaug Yacht Club closed during World War I, it was replaced by the Masons Island Yacht Club in 1927. In the following decade, despite the downturn of the national economy, which prohibited widespread participation in as expensive a hobby as yachting, interest in the sport remained high in the area, due to the arrival of G.W. Blunt White as head of the Mystic branch of Sunoco Products. Yachting afterward provided the basis for what remained of a maritime economy along the Mystic River.

Yachting, camping, artist colonies, resorts and even the casinos all served a summer population. The local population often saw these intruders as a nuisance. Helen May Clarke expressed this sentiment in her diary, writing, "This morning there were two in Main's store, saying how quaint everything was...They act as if we did not know anything and when we do they call it being trickey." She went on to relate how the summer visitors attempted to purchase her grandmother's rocking chair right from under her. When Clarke's grandmother refused to sell, on the grounds that she was

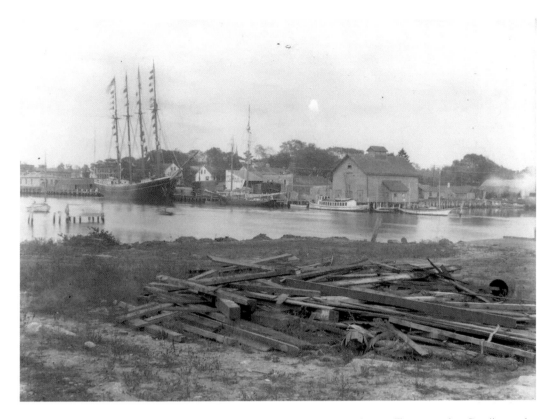

A recently launched schooner, possibly the *Marie Gilbert* launched by the Gilbert Transportation Co., lies on the east docks across from the shipyard. *Photo from Indian and Colonial Research Center, Inc., Old Mystic, Connecticut.*

using the chair and wanted to keep it, the purchasers assumed that she was simply bargaining and continued to haggle with her for some time longer. Nonetheless, much of the summer business sustained Mystic for the rest of the year, and retailers would accommodate those customers by producing Mystic-specific souvenirs and postcards.

Still, between the Civil War and World War II, most of the activity in Mystic served the community itself. The summer people might attend baseball games, horse races, plays, concerts and any one of a number of other events that took place during the summer months. They might even become seasonal members of any of the local clubs. Yet none of these events were designed specifically to attract the summer population. Sports, entertainment and civic events continued year-round and bound the residents together as a community.

Outdoor recreation, one of the main points of attraction for visitors, was also a popular means of socializing for Mystic citizens. The emphasis on good health through exercise, specifically in fresh air, as well as the invention of a variety of sports and equipment for such exercise, led to the proliferation of sports-related clubs and venues in and around Mystic. Members of such organizations as the Pequot Lodge of the Modern Woodmen of America or the Mystic Rod and Gun Club could wander the surrounding countryside and seashores for their events. Many others, however, required

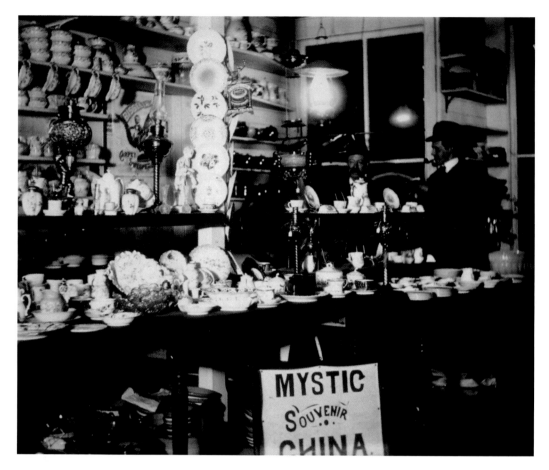

Tourism in Mystic led to a brisk business in memorabilia. Typical souvenirs of the late nineteenth and early twentieth centuries included commemorative china, such as that sold in the Thomas H. Newbury crockery and hardware store. *Mystic Seaport Collection, Mystic, Connecticut, #1980.94.72.*

open outdoor spaces for competitions, which they found at the Poquonnoc Driving Park in Groton, to the west of Mystic. The Driving Park, a half-mile oval situated on the Poquonnoc plains, occupied land owned by John Winthrop Jr. in the earliest days of colonization, but more recently by Henry Gardiner. In 1891, a company headed by Charles P. Williams and Walter Denison, who had gained some success promoting the nearby Bushy Point as a resort, leased the land from Gardiner in order to construct a racetrack. There crowds from Mystic, Groton, New London and Stonington gathered to enjoy horse, carriage and bicycle races, as well as outdoor celebrations and baseball games played on a diamond in the center of the track. The park operated from 1891 to 1900, and then again from 1908 to 1916.

The opening of the track probably contributed to the formation of clubs for two of the sports played on its grounds: bicycling and baseball. Bicycling gained enormous popularity nationwide in the 1880s. The bikes used during that decade, with their enormous front wheels, required skill and balance. In the 1890s, bikes with two evenly sized wheels operated by central pedals increased the appeal of the sport. The Mystic

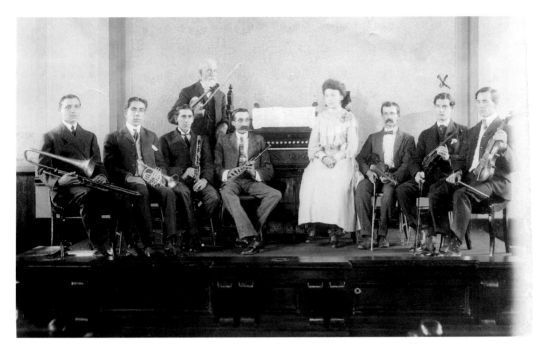

Above and below: The Burnett's Corners and Old Mystic orchestra and amateur theater troupe were among the many local entertainment groups that provided diversion in the summer and winter for both tourists and local residents. *Photos from Indian and Colonial Research Center, Inc., Old Mystic, Connecticut.*

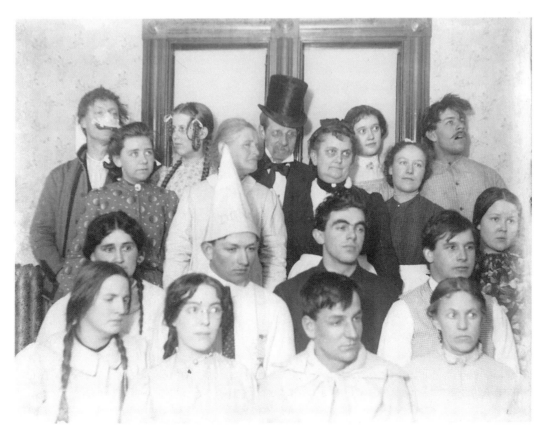

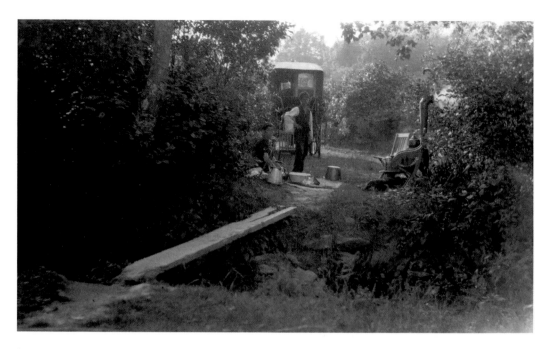

From the late nineteenth century through the 1930s, Mystic residents reported gypsy camps such as this one in the Fort Hill area, particularly during the horse racing season at the Poquonock Bridge track. Their appearance was usually met with hostility from the surrounding communities. *Photo from Indian and Colonial Research Center, Inc., Old Mystic, Connecticut.*

Wheel Club organized in 1891, joined in 1896 by the Mystic Bicycle Club. The purchase of a new bicycle was something to be noted in the newspaper, as evidenced by the mention of Ben Gaskill's purchase of "a new Butler" in 1902.

Baseball was more highly organized and widespread than cycling. As early as 1866, two amateur teams played in Mystic. The Oceanics represented Mystic River, and the Orientals played for Mystic Bridge. By 1871, the sport had developed professional leagues nationally, but smaller amateur clubs persisted. One of those amateur leagues was the Mystic Baseball Association, organized in 1891. The Oceanics and Orientals reorganized as one team, and they were joined, in 1909, by the Mystic Fat Men baseball team, boasting a total team weight of a ton. All of these teams played those from the New London Baseball Association and elsewhere. In one incident, the Mystic team rendered the Quiambaug team unable to play by luring away its six best players.

Although baseball and bicycling led to the creation of clubs, many sports were simply hobbies or pastimes in which Mystic residents participated at random. Ice skating occasionally took place on the frozen water in winter, but after 1882, a roller skating rink in Central Hall allowed people to skate year-round. Croquet also proliferated as a genteel and inexpensive game, and many pictures from the late nineteenth century show families and friends in their yards, posing with mallets and wickets.

These sports did not lead to individual organizations, but instead led to the creation of the Mystic Cosmopolitan Club, later simply the Mystic Club. The club, formed in 1911, built a facility on Holmes Street, just north of the drawbridge near the old

A RESORT COMMUNITY IN A PROGRESSIVE AGE, 1870–1940

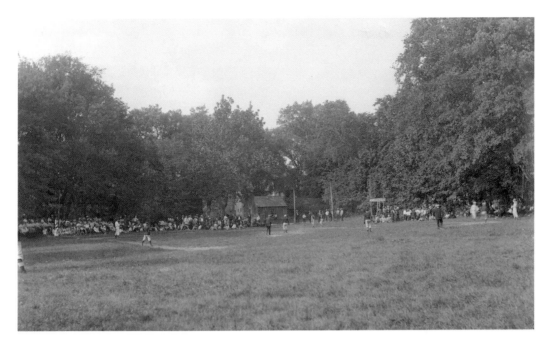

Baseball was a popular sport, among many others, in the late nineteenth century. Mystic boasted three baseball teams: the Oceanic, Oriental and Old Mystic teams. Other sports included golfing, yachting, bicycling, croquet and roller skating in the rink constructed on the second floor of Central Hall. *Photo from Indian and Colonial Research Center, Inc., Old Mystic, Connecticut.*

Mallory wharf. The building itself jutted out over the river, and members could use the club's boats or take swimming lessons. Inside, they could bowl, exercise in the gym, attend dances in the assembly hall, play billiards or engage in less strenuous activities such as whist, a card game that became a near obsession for much of the community during the winter months. Bowling, in fact, spawned smaller clubs within the larger club, such as a team that became part of the Shore Line Bowling League. The newly organized Mystic Community Club took over the building in 1921 and continued its operation for another half-century.

The winter months called for some sort of indoor entertainment. Over the decades, a series of auditoriums played host to plays, lectures, debates, pageants, recitals and concerts of all sorts. Before the Civil War, the Mystic Lyceum had sponsored such events, as had the Mystic Cornet Band, which lasted into the twentieth century. The first movie in Mystic, *Covered Wagon*, was shown to an audience in the Strand Theater in 1924. Unfortunately, the hazards of the early gas lighting and coal heat consigned each movie house to the flames. One by one, Floral Hall, Washington Hall, the Mystic Opera House, Central Hall, Mystic Theater and Strand Theater were built, burned and replaced by the next. The last, which sat adjacent to the drawbridge on East Main Street, burned in 1960. That it was not rebuilt was an indication of how Mystic's downtown economy had changed.

This focus on entertainment, however, gives a false impression of a frivolous citizenship, bent on amusement. The citizens of Mystic were, in fact, very much a

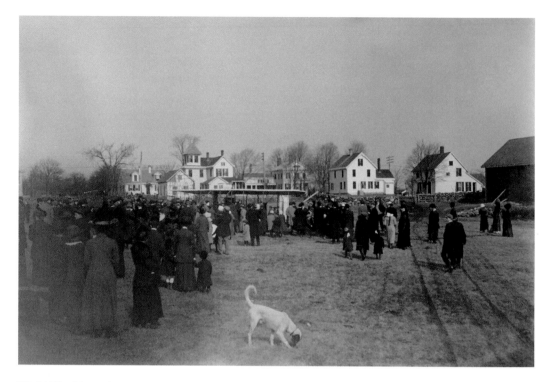

World War I brought the airplane into the popular imagination. The first plane to appear in Mystic was flown by Harry Jones in 1913, who had mistaken the Mystic River for his destination, the Thames River. His landing caused excitement, as Mystic residents flocked to the open field on the William R. Fish farm to see the amazing flying machine. *Mystic Seaport Collection, Mystic, Connecticut, #1977.3.110.*

part of the Progressive-era focus on civic organization and improvement. Most of these "Progressives" were small business owners, professionals and managers in larger companies who had benefited from industrialization, but who also felt a responsibility to control its excesses. Mystic was free from the worst problems of urbanization relative to larger towns and certainly cities, but it was not immune. The river had become polluted by industrial runoff, leading to restrictions and regulations on fishing in order to replenish the river's stock, and farming suffered financial and natural crises. Even when organizations were not aimed at a specific area of reform, they were designed to bolster patriotism and a sense of American heritage, as the native-born citizens of Anglo descent sought to define a distinctly American culture as the number of immigrants began to rival those of the native-born in coastal cities.

The earliest civic organization was actually a reaction to certain forms of entertainment in Mystic. In 1877, the Stonington Temperance Union formed in reaction to public consumption of alcohol by workingmen, and perhaps women, who populated the shipyards, factories and wharves. The owners of these enterprises, such as Thomas Greenman, naturally supported this organization. This union upheld the belief that drinking led to immoral behavior, crime, sloth and any other number of the deadly sins, to which many middle-class Americans believed the working class was particularly susceptible. The Temperance Union held well-attended lectures to educate the public on the problem and agitated for laws to prohibit the sale of alcohol. Their greatest success was the passage of a "no license" law in 1894, which prevented business establishments from obtaining a license to sell liquor. In Mystic, this merely led to greater business for saloons on the Groton side of the river, and, ultimately, the 1894 law was repealed.

Perhaps the perfect combination of entertainment and civic involvement was politics. The Whig Party, and later the Republican Party, dominated the village for the bulk of the nineteenth century, and would continue to do so into the twentieth. In 1896, the Republicans formed their own McKinley and Hobart Club, supporting industrialist William McKinley for president. By that year, however, the Democrats had made inroads. The Mystic Silver Democrats formed a Bryan and Sewell Club to support William Jennings Bryan for president. The name of their organization indicated that their primary interest in Bryan was his support of a bi-metal standard of silver and gold. The silver issue had gained popularity following the 1893 national depression. In protest, thousands of unemployed workers throughout the country staged a march on Washington. A group of these marchers, collectively known as Coxey's Army, passed through Mystic, where they were joined by Joseph Noyes, Fred Ketcham and Tony Packer. Most Democrat supporters were not quite so radical, but they continued to support Free Silver.

The 1896 presidential election was hotly contested, with Bryan appearing on the tickets of both the Democratic Party and a third party, the Populist. Historians have looked back upon his defeat as an indication of a drastic shift from an agrarian-based to an industrial-based national economy. In Mystic, that shift had clearly taken place long before, as no Populist organization of farmers appeared in the town that year.

That did not, however, mean that farmers were either passive or unorganized for their own improvement. In 1908, they organized as the Mystic Grange #171 of the Patrons of Husbandry. The Grange served a variety of functions, from agricultural education to political activism to social connection. Considered one of the most popular and active organizations in town in the 1920s, the Grange endured past the end of the twentieth century.

Business involvement in organizations took a bit longer to develop. Cooperative efforts as a business class seemed almost antithetical to the spirit of capitalism, and many industrialists were a bit suspicious of Progressive organization. From much of the period encompassed by Progressive reform, too, the economy in Mystic was in flux, with the final end of shipbuilding, the decline of manufacturing and the rise of a retail economy supplemented by the summer vacation business. By the 1930s, Mystic's role as the retail shopping center for the surrounding area had become apparent, which led to the creation of the Chamber of Commerce in 1937. At that time, the Chamber of Commerce would focus on the downtown area of Mystic, centered around the drawbridge, and support efforts to promote the retail businesses along and off Main Street.

Much earlier, in 1906, Mystic businessmen had banded together to form the Tenement Building Association. This organization was a collective effort to monitor and regulate the multifamily homes occupied by the workers of the member companies, most of

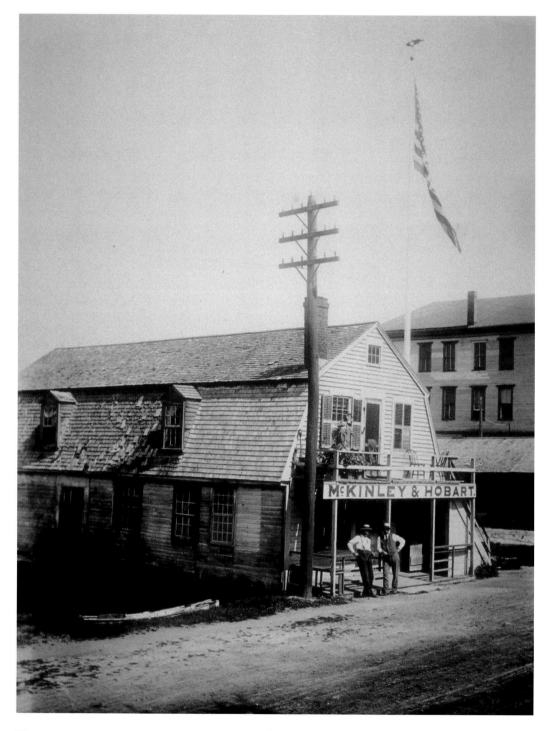

The prevalence of manufacturing in Mystic and memories of the Civil War led to widespread support of the Republican William McKinley in the 1896 election, with local Republican Party headquarters located just south of the Opera House, seen in the background, on Cottrell Street. *Mystic Seaport Collection, Mystic, Connecticut, #198041.679.*

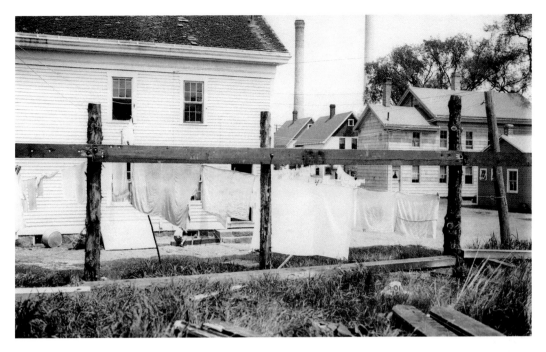

Laundry hangs out to dry behind working-class homes in Greenmanville. *Mystic Seaport Collection, Mystic, Connecticut, #1975.294.372.*

which were manufacturers. Many of these homes had originally been single-family houses, but were divided into several apartments by their owners in order to provide cheap housing for mill operatives. Even the old Seventh-Day Adventists Church in Greenmanville had been subdivided as such.

Few records of the condition of these quarters remain, but a cursory view of the surviving houses suggests cramped spaces and questionable, if not dangerous, conditions. Certainly the worst of these areas, Bogue Town, was remembered as unsanitary, unsightly and dangerous. Largely regarded as a slum, Bogue Town lay along Water Street, south of the drawbridge, near the Holmes coal yard. Water Street itself was known as "Rotten Row" because the high tide flooded the sidewalks and streets, maintaining a perpetual state of mud, algae and stench. Certainly these features extended to the homes of the people who lived between the street and the river. Helen May Clarke, that intrepid young diarist, described the area in 1919, writing, "The Bogueses live way down on the water edge, some are built out over the water. The houses they have built are shacks." As for the residents, "No one seems to know where they came from or even heard of them before the rail road was built. First a few came and lo there were a hundred."

Clarke's mention of the railroad in conjunction with the origins of Bogue Town suggests that the "Bogueses" were immigrants. In fact, many of the inhabitants of Mystic's tenements were of foreign birth, particularly around the Rossie Velvet Mill. Many native-born Americans considered immigration a problem at the turn of the nineteenth century, particularly in the major port cities. Mystic, however, was not a major port of entry, and the immigrants who arrived in the village usually came

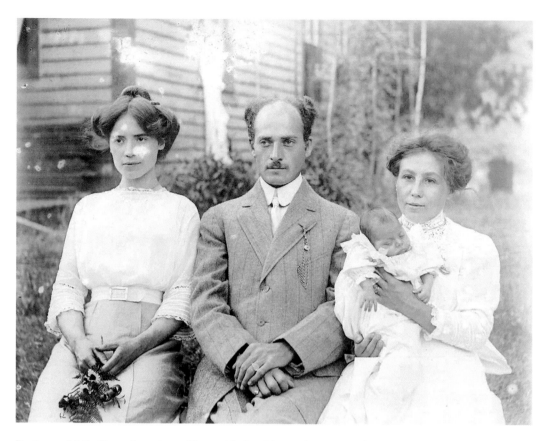

Battista and Julia Gasparino, pictured here with the oldest and youngest of their five children, emigrated from Italy to the United States around 1910. Many Italians came to the United States in the years before and after World War I, many of whom arrived in Mystic as construction workers on U.S. Highway 1. *Photo from Indian and Colonial Research Center, Inc., Old Mystic, Connecticut.*

through other means and in smaller numbers, never developing an identifiable immigrant community.

One of the largest immigrant groups in the area was the Portuguese, who began arriving in Stonington between 1863 and 1875. Generally families of fishermen, they tended to settle in Stonington Borough, which supported a large and active fishing fleet. Irish and Italians, by far the largest immigrant groups nationwide, arrived in Mystic as railroad and highway workers. Germans, however, composed the largest immigrant group in Mystic, brought over by the Rossie family to form the core of their velvet mill operatives. They, too, organized a society for purposes of singing, amusement, assimilation and celebration of their German heritage. In 1906, the society built Froshinn Hall on Greenmanville Avenue, with a beer hall on the ground level and an auditorium above.

The Mystic citizens of Anglo descent also formed societies for the improvement of their village and the preservation of its history. The earliest of these clubs was the Village Improvement League, which formed in 1899 in an effort to provide such public services as clean streets and sidewalks, as well as the general beautification of

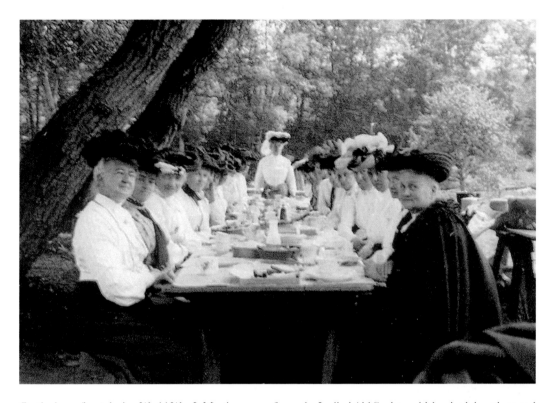

On the homefront during World War I, Mystic women formed a Ladies' Aid Society, which raised donations and rolled bandages for the war effort. During the war, Mystic residents experienced rationing, shortages, visits from sailors and soldiers on leave, rumors of spies and the Spanish influenza pandemic. *Photo from Indian and Colonial Research Center, Inc., Old Mystic, Connecticut.*

downtown. One of their earliest actions was the placement of garbage cans throughout downtown, and decades later, after the Hurricane of 1938 uprooted the majority of the trees in Mystic, the society was instrumental in their replacement. The Dahlia and Pedestrian Club, formed in 1913, and the Mystic Garden Club, formed in 1925, pursued similar beautification goals. In addition to providing horticultural education and yearly flower shows, they also promoted the preservation of the flora in and around Mystic. The Garden Club also joined with the Village Improvement League to replace the trees lost in the 1938 hurricane, and later took over the league's functions.

The same spirit of civic pride also formed the impulse for historic preservation and commemoration that emerged in the aftermath of the national centennial celebrations. Blending both the drive for beautification and the desire to commemorate the participation of Mystic in the great events of history, Mystic citizens raised several monuments around town. The earliest of these was the Liberty Pole, erected in 1862 on the west side of the river near the entrance to the drawbridge. In 1876, property disputes led to its relocation on the east side of the river. The Fanny Ledyard Chapter of the Daughters of the American Revolution also attended to the memory of the American Revolution in 1893, when they organized their mission dedicated to the placing of markers on sites of note, particularly in regard to the participation of women. Charles H. Mallory donated

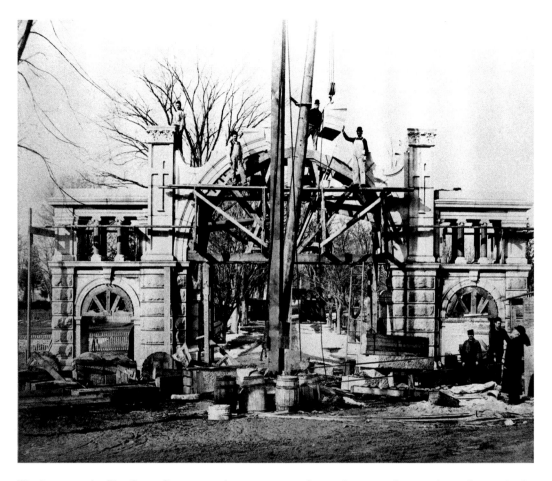

The large, granite Elm Grove Cemetery arch was constructed to replace a smaller, wooden arch, seen in the background. This cemetery was one of the first garden cemeteries in the Mystic area, modeled on Mount Auburn in Boston, Massachusetts, a cemetery that was designed as a park rather than a burial ground. *Mystic Seaport Collection, Mystic, Connecticut, #1975.294.372.*

the Civil War Soldiers' Monument that, in a disastrous opening ceremony involving a collapsed review stand and an ill-timed cannon salute, was dedicated in 1883 at the far eastern end of Main Street. A drive to raise funds for a monument to John Mason's attack on the Pequot began in 1874, and in 1889, the monument was dedicated at the intersection of Pequot Avenue and Clift Street, near the site of the fort. Waning interest in the celebration of Armistice Day, observed on November 11, led to the erection of a monument to the fallen of World War I next to the Union Baptist Church in the 1930s. These monuments stood to inscribe the history of the village into its landscape, providing daily reminders of its citizens' heritage.

Elm Grove Cemetery was related to this drive for commemoration and beautification. The cemetery had opened in 1853, located north of Greenmanville on the east bank of the river. As was typical of Victorian-era cemeteries, this one was designed as a garden rather than a burial ground. Instead of the stark rows of headstones seen in the Denison Burial Ground farther downriver, the Elm Grove Cemetery contained

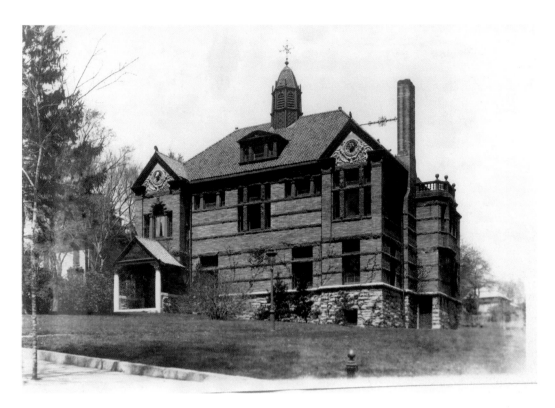

In 1891, Captain Elihu Spicer donated the funds to build the Mystic-Noank Library, which was completed in 1893, after his death. The beautiful Romanesque-style building was expanded in 1993; the work included removing a 1951 drop ceiling, which revealed the original cathedral ceiling woodwork. *Photo from Indian and Colonial Research Center, Inc., Old Mystic, Connecticut.*

winding, landscaped paths that passed clusters of family stones, which ranged from the simple soldiers' headstone to elaborate works of art. In 1895, an elaborate stone arch was donated by the widow of Charles H. Mallory in his memory. It replaced an older wooden arch that had also served as the cemetery entrance. In this way, Mystic citizens could bring their own individual ancestors into the historical landscape.

Yet the preservation of Mystic's history required more than monuments and memorials, and historical societies organized to preserve buildings and collect documents and artifacts from Mystic's past. To that end, the Road Society and the Stonington Historical Society organized in 1895, but most associations for this sort of historical preservation did not form until the late 1920s and 1930s, prompted by the tricentennial celebration of Connecticut's founding, and with as much an eye to attracting out-of-town visitors as to preservation. Beginning in 1929, with the establishment of the Marine Historical Association, the 1930s saw the foundation of the Denison Society and the Fort Hill Indian Museum. The last, under the direction of anthropologist Eva L. Butler, only lasted three years, but served as the foundation for the later Indian and Colonial Research Center that opened in Old Mystic in 1965. All of these historical organizations became part of the next phase of Mystic's economic history, that of historic tourism.

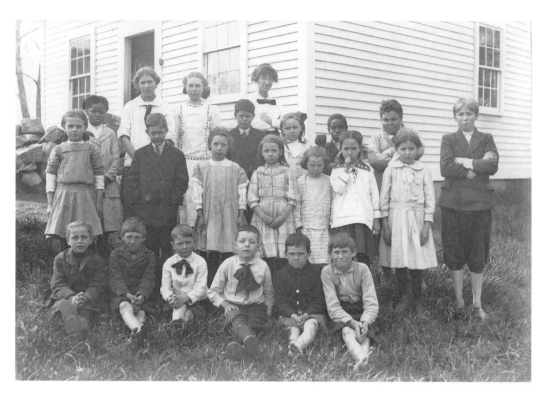

Ellen Brown's class, in Old Mystic, demonstrated racial integration at a time when segregation was the norm. *Photo from Indian and Colonial Research Center, Inc., Old Mystic, Connecticut.*

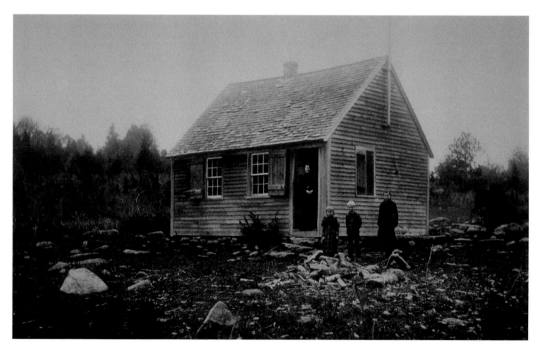

The Fishtown school, a one-room schoolhouse west of Mystic, was typical of the types of educational institutions attended by the children in the rural areas around Mystic. *Mystic Seaport Collection, Mystic, Connecticut, #1977.92.53.*

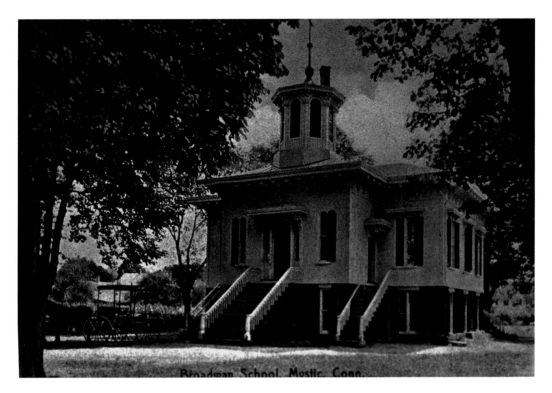

The Broadway school, a public school located on the Stonington side of the river. *Mystic Seaport Collection, Mystic, Connecticut, #1993.17.617.*

These historical societies also functioned as venues for public education, a subject that received much attention in the late nineteenth century. As with all other Progressive community developments, libraries were seen as a means of improving citizenship for both the native-born and immigrant populations. In Mystic, most community organizations, such as the Mystic Club, incorporated libraries into their facilities. The community itself, however, constructed a large public library through the beneficence of Captain Elihu Spicer. Spicer had been a business partner of Charles H. Mallory, and had traveled the globe throughout the nineteenth century. Just before his death in 1891, he donated the funds for the construction of an elegant two-story building on Library Street, just north of West Main Street, which opened in 1894.

The first high school opened in the mid-nineteenth century, with the Portersville Academy beginning classes in 1838 and the Mystic Academy in 1852. Although the latter failed after only a few years as a private school, it reopened as a public school. In 1909, the Broadway School opened on the east side of the river, and in 1910, a newer Mystic Academy opened on the west side. Public high schools were more successful, with one opening in Mystic River and one in West Mystic in 1872. Both, along with schools in Burnett's Corners, Noank and Poquonnoc, were finally consolidated into a single school district in 1941.

Mystic also provided education to hearing impaired students at the Mystic Oral School. The Mystic Oral School was established by the Whipple family in 1870,

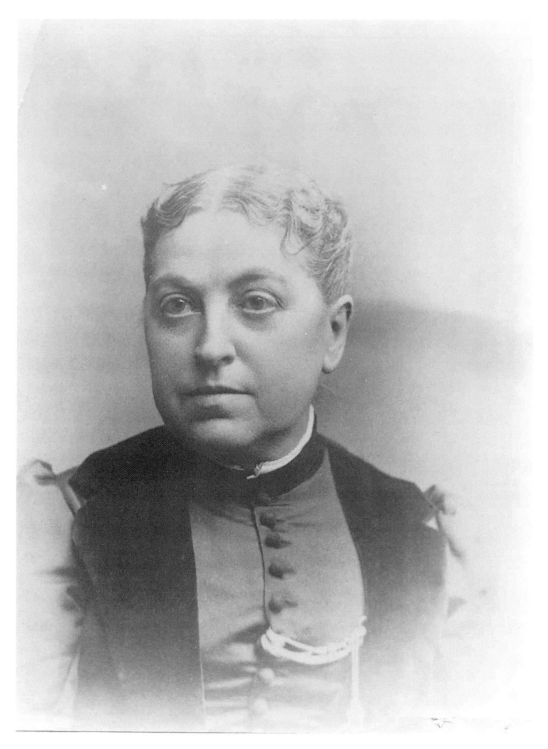

Many widowed women, as well as families, opened their homes to boarders in order to earn extra income for the household. Mary Starr, wife of sea captain Norman Starr, opened her Groton home to teacher Lillian Ingram. *Photo from Indian and Colonial Research Center, Inc., Old Mystic, Connecticut.*

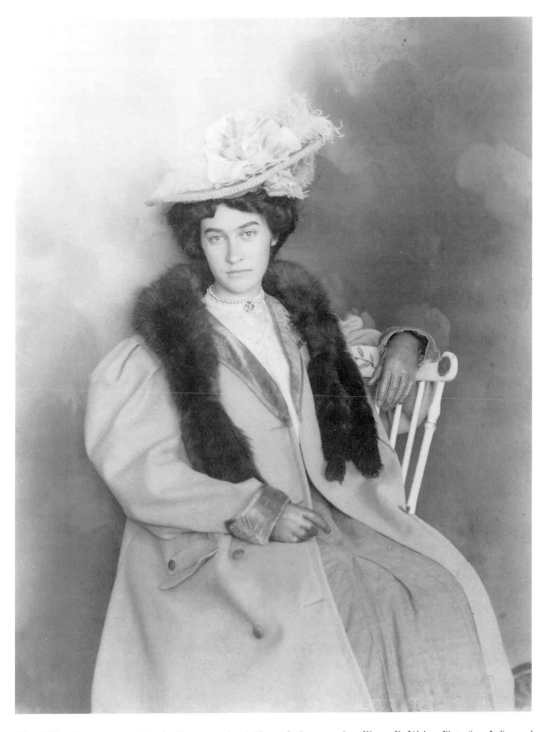

Miss Lillian Ingram, a teacher in Groton and neighbor of photographer Elmer E. Waite. *Photo from Indian and Colonial Research Center, Inc., Old Mystic, Connecticut.*

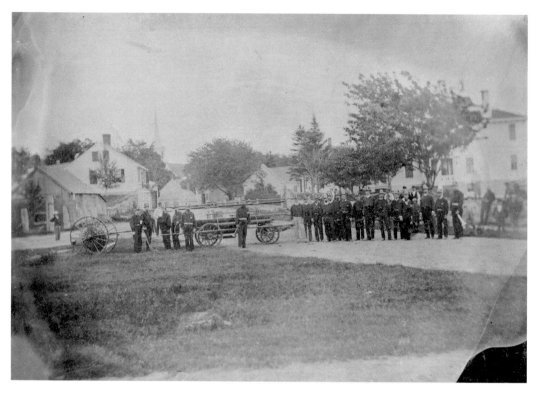

In 1837, the residents of Old Mystic established the first fire company in the Mystic area with a hand-drawn fire pumper, called "Reliance," shown in this picture. The lower villages found that the distance from Old Mystic was too far for Reliance to respond quickly to emergencies, and established their own companies just a few years later. *Photo from Indian and Colonial Research Center, Inc., Old Mystic, Connecticut.*

eventually occupying the mansion once owned by Silas E. Burrows. Originally named the Whipple Home School for Deaf Mutes, after its founder, the name changed in 1895 to reflect a new emphasis on oral communication for the deaf. Alexander Graham Bell, whose mother and wife were both deaf, and whose experiments in inventing a device to help the deaf speak produced the telephone, endorsed the school himself in 1903. The school remained in operation until 1980.

In the late nineteenth and early twentieth centuries, Mystic also became a modernized town. Public utilities became available starting in 1879, and the creation of the first permanent fire companies came as well. Running water, gas and electricity reached private homes, and new technology for communication, mass transportation and improved roads connected Mystic to surrounding towns.

Fires had always been a problem in Mystic, as evidenced by the constant replacement of theaters that had been destroyed by flames. One errant spark could destroy an entire shipyard, factory or downtown block, spelling disaster for owners, employees and residents. Old Mystic had a fire department, including a hand pump, as early as 1837. Mystic Bridge and Portersville, however, could not rely upon this company. By the time a fire had been reported and the pump traveled over the poorly surfaced road, the threatened building would have been lost, along with several others. This scenario

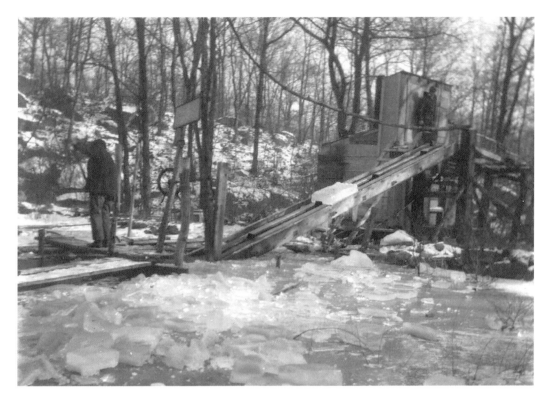

Until the widespread use of the electric refrigerator well into the twentieth century, Mystic residents relied upon ice cut from surrounding ponds during the winter. Here, two workers collect ice on Beebe's pond, on the west side of the Mystic River near Noank. *Photo from Indian and Colonial Research Center, Inc., Old Mystic, Connecticut.*

occurred in 1858, when the block between East Main Street, Holmes Street and the river went up in flames.

The first successful fire company to form in the lower Mystic villages was the Mystic Bridge Fire Engine Company in 1846, which only lasted for a few years. Another fire company, Mazeppa #1, named for its engine, was located on Holmes Street. In 1875, the first permanent company was the B.F. Hoxie Steam Fire Engine Company, named in honor of the generous donations of Benjamin F. Hoxie, who owned a considerable amount of property around the engine house. In 1878, dissention in the Hoxie Company ranks led to the creation of the Mystic Hook and Ladder Company across the river. A year later, these two private companies became tax-supported organizations with the creation of the Mystic Fire District by the Connecticut State Legislature. In 1915, the district installed a town fire alarm system, which was followed by the creation of a fire police force in 1922 and the purchase of a radio in 1924.

Public utilities that affected everyday life arrived in Mystic during the 1880s and 1890s, although they all remained in private hands. The Mystic Water Company began supplying running water to the wealthiest of homes in 1887. In its earliest days, it supplied water to cisterns in the attics of homes, where gravity would bring the water down pipes to the rest of the house. Gradually, as plumbing improved, the company

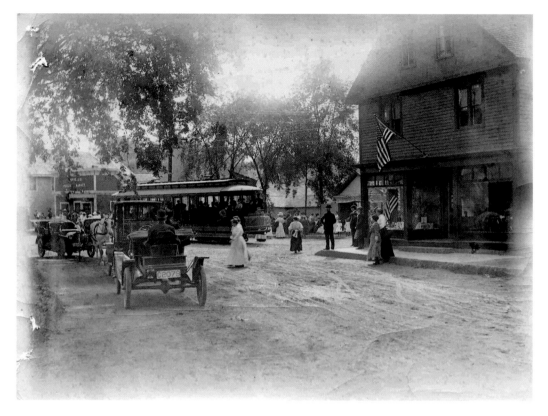

In 1904, trolleys became the first public transportation in Mystic. The first line connected the ferry on the Thames River in Groton to the Pawcatuck River on the Rhode Island border, crossing the Mystic River bridge in between. That line was connected to Old Mystic in 1911, as shown here. *Photo from Indian and Colonial Research Center, Inc., Old Mystic, Connecticut.*

was able to supply a greater number of customers. In 1889, the Mystic Electric Light and Gas Company started business, becoming the Mystic Power Company in 1907. Electricity was such a marvel and welcome source of power that even the wiring of a business or home was a thing of note in the newspapers.

New technology in communication took a little longer to appeal to the public in Mystic. The 1854 county map shows a telegraph office here, and in 1889, the first Western Union Telegraph office opened in the Hoxie House Hotel, but efforts to wire the region with telephones met with early failures. About the same time, the Southern New England Telephone Company offered service to a handful of homes in Mystic, but the telephones failed to catch on with other customers and the service was discontinued in 1890. In 1895, the company tried again, with more success. Thirty buildings had telephones installed, and an exchange building appeared near the railway depot. Over the next two decades, the telephone infiltrated the homes and businesses throughout Mystic.

The arrival of electricity permitted a trolley system that allowed the people of Mystic to travel much more quickly to the Thames and Pawcatuck Rivers. The Groton and Stonington Street Railway began operating in 1904, with the trolley

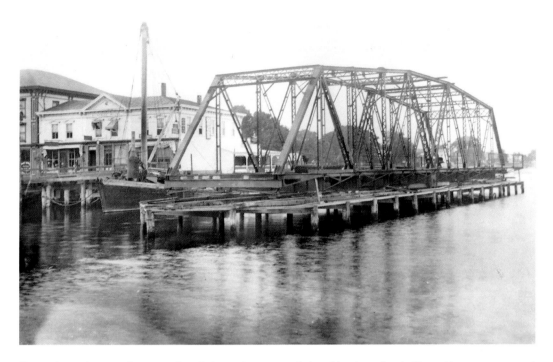

The weight of the trolley necessitated the replacement of the older iron drawbridge with a stronger, steel drawbridge, shown here in its open position in 1904. The building in the background housed a popular ice cream shop. *Photo from Indian and Colonial Research Center, Inc., Old Mystic, Connecticut.*

electric generating powerhouse and barn located on Water Street in Mystic. In 1911, an extension line ran up to Old Mystic and another down to Noank. Mary Virginia Goodman recalled riding the trolley each morning from Noank to Groton Heights Grammar School in the early twentieth century, and declared, "The trolley was reliable, convenient and we considered it a fine means of transportation." Mystic inhabitants, hosts to visitors from other towns, could now themselves become the guests, taking day trips to New London and Stonington for visits to the beach, movies or friends and relatives.

The trolleys led to problems with the drawbridge, however. The rotating iron bridge erected in 1866 was designed to support the weight of carriages and wagons, not the weight of trolleys, and was completely rebuilt in 1904. By the end of World War I, cars joined the trolleys, stressing the bridge to its limit. As a result, a bascule bridge replaced the iron bridge in 1922. This type of bridge design was well suited to the shallow Mystic River because it placed the counterweights above the bridge. This drawbridge continues in use to this day.

While passengers such as Goodman might have enjoyed the trolleys, the men who drove them were not so enamored. Exposure to the elements, even after the cars were closed during the winters, and low wages drove them to threaten a strike in 1914, and to go on strike in 1916 and 1919. All disputes were settled with a pay increase. Within a decade, however, buses replaced the trolley. Cars, in turn, rendered the buses obsolete by the 1950s.

Indeed, cars, highways and interstates would all facilitate Mystic's transformation into a tourist destination. Modernized public utilities had certainly assisted in the appeal of Mystic as a destination for vacationers and summer residents, and the roads would be no different. While Mystic had survived the disappearing shipbuilding industry, and watched as manufacturing declined, its residents had adjusted to their conditions by providing themselves and their guests with diversions, improving their town and preserving their history. That last bit would enable Mystic to thrive over the next half-century.

CHAPTER 7

TOURIST TOWN, 1940–2001

On November 8, 1941, a bedraggled wooden whaling ship made her way up the Mystic River, towed by a U.S. Coast Guard cutter. Passing through the opened bascule bridge, she trailed her escort up to Adams Point, where she came to her final resting place at the Marine Historical Association grounds. The date of her arrival was fortuitous. A month later and the coast guard would have been unable to spare a vessel for towing, as by then they were requiring all ships to patrol American waters, on the lookout for German or Japanese subs. This ship, the *Charles W. Morgan*, would find new life as the centerpiece of the association's museum and, in turn, help to give new life to Mystic's economy when World War II had ended.

By 1940, Mystic had seen life as a Pequot village, an outlying colonial settlement, a shelter in imperial wars, a center for shipbuilding, a small manufacturing town and a resort community. In the inter-war years, manufacturing had all but disappeared from the town, leaving an economy based largely upon the retail business of the surrounding communities. Resorts and casinos closed down, unable to recover from the business lost in World War I and the Depression, but artists and vacationers continued to flock to the town in the summer months. Additionally, the year-round Mystic residents had taken to beautifying their community and preserving its history. Faster and more efficient transportation, which allowed more and more Americans to travel farther and farther from home on inexpensive outings, would allow Mystic to combine its preexisting status as a summer destination with the growing interest in historic preservation in order to create an economy based on tourism, specifically historical or heritage tourism. The construction of I-95 would inaugurate the peak years of tourism, lasting through the 1960s, 1970s and 1980s; the re-emergence of the Pequot nation would signal the changing nature of tourism regionally at the century's end.

Road improvements and historical preservation efforts of the 1920s and '30s had laid the groundwork for this transformation into a tourist town. As early as 1891, the Connecticut State Legislature had appointed a commission to improve roads

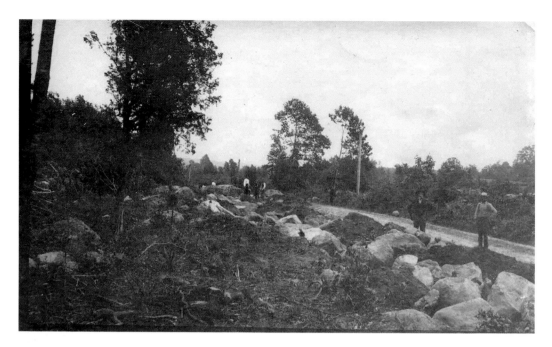

The Great War underscored the need for improved roads and led to government funding of highway improvements. Here, the road through Groton between the Thames and the Mystic Rivers is straightened, leveled and paved. This became part of U.S. Highway 1. *Photo from Indian and Colonial Research Center, Inc., Old Mystic, Connecticut.*

and highways, an action that became more urgent as automobiles came into use in the following two decades. Cars and motor tourists had appeared on Mystic roads by 1908, when a car from Philadelphia struck a seven-year-old boy. Fortunately, the boy was unharmed, as the car was only traveling seven miles per hour. World War I demonstrated the dangerously poor and inconsistent conditions of national roads as the armed forces attempted to transport men and materiel across country. In the interest of both national security and cross-country trade, the U.S. government passed the Federal Highway Act of 1921. This act provided for a system of modern highways connecting all states. Along the East Coast, federal funds improved a series of state and local highways, and incorporated them into U.S. Route 1. In Mystic, the Old New London Road, East and West Main Streets and the Mystic River drawbridge would all become part of this early interstate highway.

The biggest obstacle faced by the road workers when they arrived in town in 1923 was the crooked public way from the Old New London Road at the top of Baptist Hill to the drawbridge across the river. Originally, the road had run to a ferry at the foot of the hill, but later the bridge had been built at the foot of what became West Main Street, several hundred yards north of the ferry landing. The early road builders had simply re-routed traffic by connecting the terminus to West Main Street with a stretch of Water Street. This put two right angles in the road, something that would stall traffic on U.S. Route 1. Additionally, the hill, named for the white-steepled Union Baptist Church crowning the town, had a very steep grade that overpowered

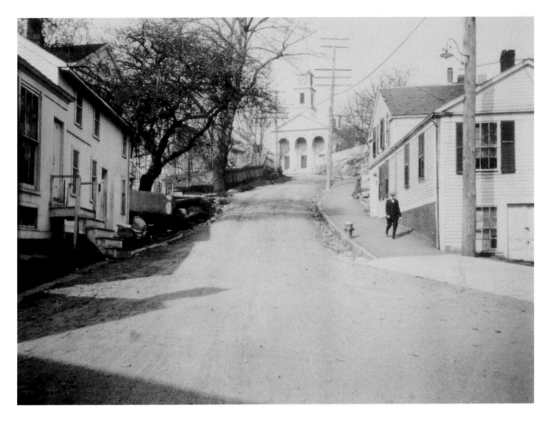

The grade of Baptist Hill was too steep for early automobile engines to easily climb in 1911, when New London Road was to be connected to West Main Street as part of U.S. Highway 1. At that time, the road was level with the Union Baptist Church at the top of the hill. *Mystic Seaport Collection, Mystic, Connecticut, #1946.623.7.*

the engines of these early automobiles. To eliminate both problems, the road builders cut a spur from the Old New London Road to West Main Street at the top of the hill, beside the church. They then blasted into the hill to lower the grade of the road. This left the church sitting on a ledge, presiding over the town.

The construction of U.S. Route 1 provided jobs for many local men and allowed faster passage through the village. Mystic residents could commute to work farther away more easily, and as manufacturing and shipbuilding moved to Stonington Borough, Groton and New London, workers could follow without being uprooted. That they continued to live in Mystic meant that Mystic merchants could retain their businesses and benefit from regional economic development, even if that development did not occur specifically in Mystic itself.

Similarly, the highway brought more and more visitors through Mystic, providing an incentive for Mystic citizens, particularly merchants, to convince them to stop, if only for a few hours. All of New England, and indeed the nation, underwent a similar process. Businesses began to encourage their workers to take vacations, paying higher wages and offering time off. They particularly encouraged weekend driving excursions or tours of the countryside because the use of automobiles stimulated so many ancillary

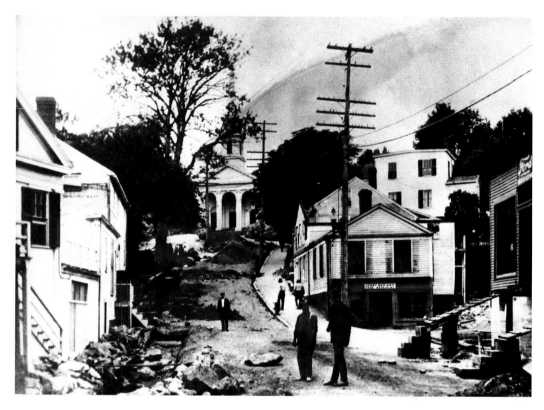

In constructing U.S. Highway 1, the grade of West Main Street was lowered, leaving the Union Baptist Church perched above the town on a cliff, and cutting through parts of the backyards of houses to the south. *Mystic Seaport Collection, Mystic, Connecticut, #1959.86.*

industries. In New England, many towns realized that this tourist business could help alleviate the local depressions that so many had experienced in the previous decades. The main commodities they had to offer were rural settings and local history.

In Mystic, the preexisting interest in preserving local history dovetailed with this desire to attract visitors. Initially, historic preservation focused on the collection of documents and artifacts and the presentation of academic lectures on historical subjects. This was the original mission of both the Stonington Historical Society, founded in 1895, and the Marine Historical Association, founded in 1929. Local historians soon realized that if they displayed these items, they could attract visitors who would be willing to pay admission to see these remnants of the past.

The unwitting pioneer of museums in Mystic was Charles Q. Eldredge. A native of Mystic, where he retired in 1917, Eldredge had collected over seven hundred curios, ranging from charred Indian bones found on his property in Mystic to an entire whale skeleton. On his River Road estate, he built a small museum where he displayed these artifacts, requesting a small donation and offering a catalogue of his collection for thirty-five cents. In 1918, he boasted five hundred visitors. The Charles Q. Eldredge Museum was a private affair, however, and closed upon his death in 1930. His collection disappeared into the hands of enthusiasts when it was sold in pieces at auction.

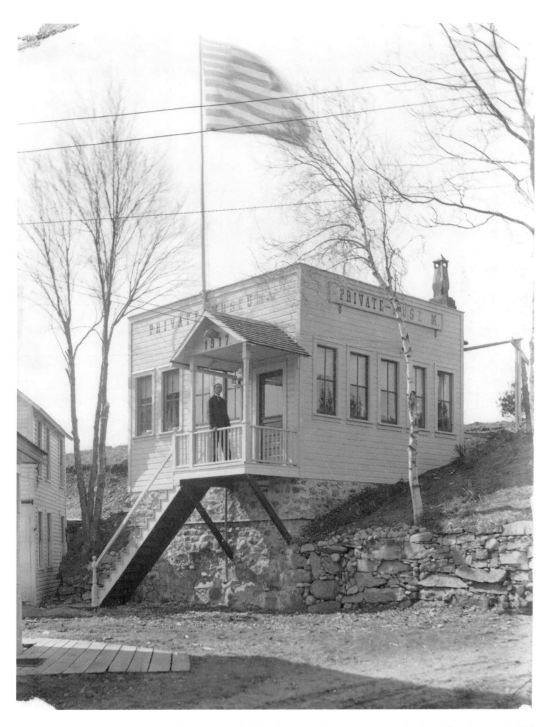

Charles Q. Eldredge opened the first museum in Mystic along the northwestern bank of the river near Old Mystic. Following the model of nineteenth-century museums, he displayed his personal collection of curiosities, which included local Native American bones and artifacts, in this small building and on its grounds, and sold a small catalogue of its items. *Photo from Indian and Colonial Research Center, Inc., Old Mystic, Connecticut.*

By that time, historical organizations began to see the potential for museums as permanent institutions. The Denison Society, established in 1930, may have dedicated itself to the history of a single family, but the proliferation of that family since the 1660s married its history to that of the region. In 1941, when Ann Borodell Denison Gates, the last inhabitant of the 1717 Denison homestead, died, she left the property to the society. The society restored the building, using each room to present a different period in the history of the house; the museum opened in 1947.

Whereas the Denison Society took a focused view of a particular family in Mystic, the Marine Historical Association dedicated itself to the preservation of all maritime history. Mystic history itself was not specified, but the maritime history of Mystic composed the basis for its collections, due to the availability of materials and the participation of the descendants of the major Mystic shipbuilders. The association acquired its first buildings, the woolen factories of the Mystic Manufacturing Company, which were restored as exhibit halls. The first building opened with exhibits of maritime artifacts in 1931, followed by a much larger exhibition building named for the grandson of Clark Greenman, Charles K. Stillman, who was one of the three founders of Mystic Seaport. By then, the association had begun proceedings to acquire the *Charles W. Morgan* from a New Bedford organization that could no longer afford to restore the vessel.

A less successful but no less notable museum opened in 1935. Eva L. Butler had moved to Mystic in 1928 and quickly became active in local history. She became curious about the Native Americans in the area and educated herself on their past. In 1935, she organized the Fort Hill Indian Memorial Association to construct a museum on the site where the fort of Sassacus had sat at the time of the Pequot War. This was not the fort that had been burned by the English, but the one that lay farther south, on the edge of the Poquonnoc plain. The association built a replica of a log cabin on the crest of Fort Hill, along Route 1, and displayed the Native American artifacts that Butler had acquired. Unfortunately, financial difficulties led to the closing of the museum in 1937. World War II dashed the association's hope to reopen the museum, and the building stood decaying until a storm blew it down in 1979.

Butler was one of three women whose contributions to Mystic history cannot be overlooked. This trio included Butler, Grace Denison Wheeler and Carol W. Kimball. The earliest of these three historians was Wheeler, who had been born in Stonington in 1858. She dedicated much of her life to recording and researching the history and old homes of Stonington. In particular, her book *Old Homes in Stonington* (1900) became an influential reference source long after her death in 1956.

Despite the failure of the Fort Hill museum, Eva Butler continued to research Mystic's history, compiling volumes of information from primary sources concerning the Native American and early English population. Toward the end of her life, in an effort to preserve her work, she organized the Indian and Colonial Research Center. The center purchased the old Mystic National Bank building in Old Mystic to house her collection, and it would become instrumental in preserving Mystic's history, particularly that of its native people.

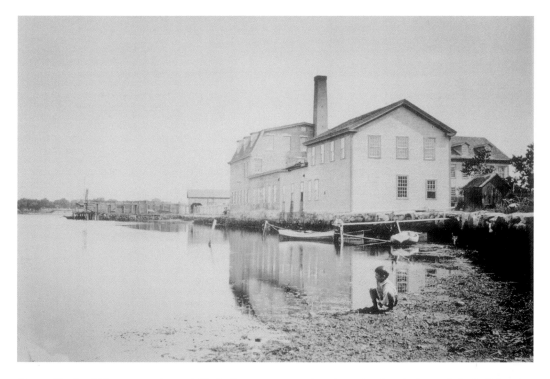

Young Charles Stillman, grandson of Clark Greenman, crouches along the river in front of the building that would later bear his name. Stillman and other family members inherited the Greenman property, including the shipyard and the mill complex pictured here, and then donated it to the Marine Historical Association. *Mystic Seaport Collection, Mystic, Connecticut, #1975.294.267.*

Carol W. Kimball was among the founders of the Indian and Colonial Research Center. She had arrived in Mystic during the Depression and quickly became fascinated with its history. She began writing a history column for the *New London Day*, and became a valued consultant to all of the historical organizations that arose in Mystic for the rest of the century. Her prolific local publications reveal a wealth of information about the history of the area. Together, these three women have preserved not only the history of Mystic, but also the integrity of the research that underlies the representation of that history.

By World War II, the two major factors that would influence Mystic's development in the postwar years were in place. The war and, more importantly, its aftermath would accelerate the town's growth into a tourist center, as historical tourism became a tool in the cultural war against Communism and a means to exploit both the prosperity of the early Cold War years and the demand to entertain the swelling numbers of children produced in the baby boom. The interstate highway system sped this process, bringing more people from farther away who wanted to see or show their children what life was like "back then."

Mary Virginia Goodman, a schoolteacher in Noank at the time, gave an ominous description of the beginning of World War II along the Mystic River. On December 8, 1941, "a call was sent out from the town school office to all the

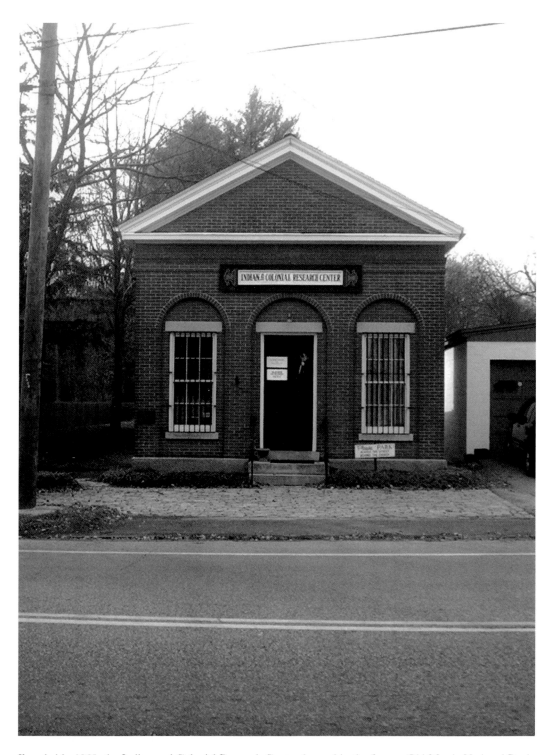

Founded in 1965, the Indian and Colonial Research Center, housed in the former Old Mystic National Bank, preserves Mystic anthropologist Eva L. Butler's collection of Native American artifacts, local history and genealogical records. *Photo by author, 2006.*

schools to close the schools at once, send the pupils home or to a neighbors' if the mothers were not at home," Goodman wrote. "The reason given sent chills into every hearer, pupil and teacher alike," she continued. "The school office had been warned that enemy planes were seen advancing toward our shores." This was not the case, but no rumor was dismissed during this time of crisis, and the entire East Coast from Maine to Florida entered a "dim out" at night for the duration of the war. With a U.S. Coast Guard station on Avery Point in Groton, a navy submarine base on the Thames River and army pilots stationed at Trumbull airfield just south of Poquonnoc Bridge, military personnel and maneuvers became a regular feature of life around Mystic.

The war brought not only more soldiers and sailors to the Mystic area, but also more companies involved in military production and employees to staff their production lines. During the war, Electric Boat expanded its capacity by constructing a second shipyard, called the Victory Yard, a mile south of their main shipyard. Here they launched a total of seventy-four submarines and employed over two thousand people. Between the military personnel and the shipyard employees, most of whom brought their families, the population of Groton doubled during the 1940s, drastically taxing local, state and federal resources for housing, schools and basic utilities. Fort Hill Homes, a federal housing project to build temporary homes for employees of military-related industries, sprang up on the site of the former Poquonnoc Driving Park. The houses were reserved, with long waiting lists, before many of the homes were constructed. While some small shops, and even nightclubs to cater to the single—or circumstantially single—sailors appeared between Groton and Mystic, Mystic received much of the shopping business of this population growth.

When the war ended, most people in the country expected a return to the Depression; that certainly would have been the case in Mystic had the shipyards closed or scaled back production. Instead, the continued emphasis on military production as part of the Cold War and the arrival of the Pfizer pharmaceutical factory in Groton caused a profound stabilization in the regional economy for several decades after the war. The population growth leveled, with the baby boom being the major source of increase for the next decade and a half. These growing families demanded permanent and larger homes, leading to a boom in housing construction supplemented by federal incentives to build suburbs.

Between 1945 and 1965, Mystic itself became an outlying suburb of Groton and New London. The town provided a center for shopping for much of that time, and the town merchants banded together in 1946 to form the Mystic Merchants' Association to address parking problems downtown and customers' demands for regular and consistent working hours. Retail business thrived, only taking a slight blow when malls began to appear on Route 1, nearer to the center of population in Groton.

The Cold War affected the promotion of historical or heritage tourism as well. The war had necessarily led to a drop in the tourist business. Afterward, after fifteen years of economic depression and rationing, Americans now found themselves in possession of discretionary funds that permitted vacations. As their children became old enough to travel, parents went in search of interesting places to take them for vacation. Many Americans, with a little prompting by those running the sites, saw excursions to historical locations as a means of providing their children with an education in civics. Such vacations would demonstrate to them the grandeur and progress of American history, providing a bulwark against Communism and ensuring the perpetuation of democracy.

In Mystic, the societies and organizations that ran the local historic museums also felt that increase in funds that had been so scarce in the past fifteen years. Route 1 continued to bring in tourists, and Mystic responded, capitalizing on the very same things that had brought visitors to the town for over half a century. While the most successful and visible of the efforts centered on historical tourism, the natural environment also constituted part of the region's attraction, especially in an era when most people considered the wilderness itself a thing of the past.

By mid-century, a concern with the impact of industry and modern life on the natural environment had emerged. In an effort to combat the destruction of various species and ecosystems, to provide environmental education and to present the public with a glimpse of relatively untouched nature, organizations formed to open parks and preserves. These preserves were of particular interest because the New England countryside that had been familiar to many generations was bare, deforested by centuries of farming and logging, and postwar development threatened new growth.

In Mystic, two nature preserves opened to visitors after World War II. In 1946, the Mystic Garden Club, still offering horticultural lectures and flower shows, acquired property from the Denison family to open the Denison Pequotsepos Nature Center. Mary L. Jobe, now the widow of explorer Carl Ackley, still owned the old peace meeting grounds, site of her girls' camp in the early part of the century. When she died in 1966, she donated the property for a nature preserve. Earlier, in 1951, she had also donated Mystic Island as a wildlife sanctuary. The Thames Science Center, which had received both of these donations, had been founded in part through the efforts of Eva L. Butler. As its mission began to focus on mechanical sciences, the Pequotsepos Center took over the management of both Mystic Island and the Peace Sanctuary. In Mystic, while the river would always draw boaters, with yacht races resuming in 1946, two local preserves began to offer visitors something natural, new and fragile.

This natural environment that had so appealed to artists continued to do so. The Mystic Art Association began to hold annual shows and, beginning in 1958, an Outdoor Art Festival. This latter event attracted both local and out-of-town artists. Held in August and advertised in the *New York Times*, the annual festival allowed artists to display their work as a preview of winter shows or to garner the attention of gallery owners. The festival also coincided with the peak of the summer tourist season, flooding the town with artists, agents, critics, gallery owners and families, and thereby boosting the business of motels and restaurants as well as all other local attractions.

The Marine Historical Association, however, took the most ambitious steps in regard to tourism. Originally, the association had planned simply to collect artifacts and documents relating to maritime history, but it soon acquired the old Greenman woolen factory buildings, where its museum opened in 1931. The arrival of the *Charles*

W. Morgan in 1941 suggested greater possibilities for its future as part of a trend toward outdoor, living history museums.

Outdoor history museums offered an immersive experience of the past. Colonial Williamsburg set the standard and precedent for such a museum when it opened in 1934. Thus, when the *Morgan* arrived on the Marine Historical Association's grounds in 1941, the association saw the opportunity to expand its mission. Combining the examples of Old Sturbridge Village and Greenfield, Michigan, the association began to construct a seaport village by acquiring and moving various buildings and vessels from throughout New England to the abandoned property of the old Greenman shipyard adjacent to the mill complex. Throughout the 1940s, beginning with the *Morgan*, the association expanded its collection through purchases and donations. The museum became such a regional attraction that a 1958 proposal to coordinate the activities and advertisements of various historic New England sites, called "Yankee Homecoming," featured the association as a key stop.

As the association's seaport began to transform Mystic into a prominent destination, the tourist trade throughout the entire nation was being transformed by the construction of the interstate highway system. Much as after World War I, the federal government began to see highways as key to national security. The number of automobiles and their owners' willingness to use them taxed the existing highway system. Thus, Congress passed the Federal Highway Act in 1955 and the Interstate Highway Act in 1956. Interstate 95, paralleling Route 1, would connect the cities on the entire eastern seaboard but follow a more direct path, bypassing most towns in order to alleviate traffic. The plans for the interstate route through Groton and Stonington showed the highway as passing between Old Mystic and Mystic, on the northern edge of Elm Grove Cemetery. Two exits, numbered 89 and 90, put traffic off on Allyn Street on the west side of the river and Greenmanville Avenue on the east side of the river.

Mystic was fortunate in the placement of the interstate. Many cities lost large historic districts, and the placement of interstates was used to reinforce *de facto* Jim Crow segregation. This occurred not only in the South, but also as close to Mystic as Bridgeport, New Haven and Pawtucket. Ethnically and racially homogenous, with its poorer neighborhoods lying much farther south than the interstate, Mystic escaped the social strife experienced in other communities. Additionally, because the path of the interstate ran largely through farmland, few historic sites were affected. Even then, the Stonington Historical Society stepped in and purchased Whitehall Manor, the single major structure in the path of the highway, and moved the building a hundred yards to the north, next to the exit ramp, for use as its library. The Marine Historical Association also rescued a building in the path of the highway when it purchased the Buckingham Hall house and moved it from Saybrook to the museum grounds in 1958.

The exits from the interstate were the greatest problems created by its construction. Although the Allyn Street exit offered the least complicated route to downtown Mystic, as well as to Noank and the summer homes on Groton Long Point, the Greenmanville Avenue exit would become the focal point for tourist development. In 1972, Olde Mistick Village, a cluster of shops in buildings meant to resemble a prototypical quaint town, opened on the south side of the interstate, on the east side

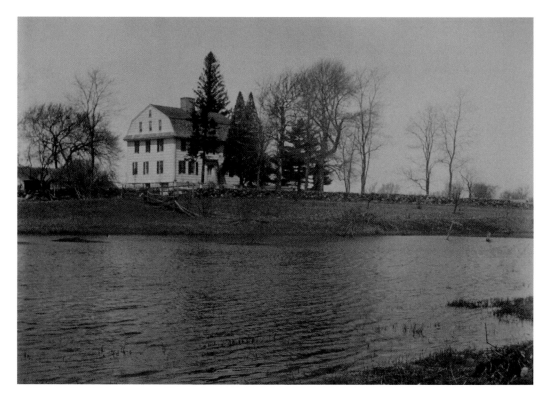

Whitehall Mansion, built by Dr. Dudley Woodbridge in the early eighteenth century, in its original location. The building was moved approximately one hundred yards north in the 1960s to save it from the construction of I-95. At one time it was owned by the Stonington Historical Society and was open to the public. *Mystic Seaport Collection, Mystic, Connecticut, #1994.18.10.*

of Greenmanville Avenue. Two years later, in the same area, the Mystic Aquarium opened and proved so popular that it expanded in the 1980s. Most of the traffic to Mystic, however, took the Allyn Street exit, clogging the streets of downtown and interfering with residential traffic.

To solve the problem, in 1979, the word "Mystic" was removed from the Allyn Street exit sign, and all tourist traffic was routed to exit 90. Through the 1980s and 1990s, major hotel and fast food chains serving Mystic opened at this intersection. By the end of the century, real estate developers, catering to commuters to as far away as Providence and a demand for summer residences, constructed modern subdivisions north of the highway. Thirty years after the sign change, exit 90 would be the hook in a proposed regional advertising campaign.

The interstate was the major asset to the development of Mystic as a tourist center, particularly in the 1970s. The interstate made Mystic a convenient destination during the bicentennial celebrations of 1976, which caused a boom in heritage tourism throughout the country, particularly in areas that contained some connection to the colonial and Revolutionary eras. Indeed, this peak in tourism to historic sites would haunt museums for decades afterward as they attempted to regain that level of visitation in the face of changing tourism trends.

The bicentennial also stimulated the creation of historic districts, supported by federal funding that encouraged historic preservation in urban areas as an alternative to razing historic districts. Much like the construction of the interstate highways, the creation of historic districts often dislocated the generally poverty-stricken people who had filled the vacancies left by suburban migration. Residents interested in establishing historic districts in Mystic, however, responded to a complicated set of issues.

They honestly hoped to improve the appearance of their town and homes, regardless of outside influences. Most of the people living in Mystic were middle-class residents of modest means who lacked the extra income required for the restoration of their homes. Federal grants would permit not only the restoration of their homes to their original appearances, retaining the historic character of the neighborhood, but also the modernization of badly outdated or dangerous plumbing and electrical systems.

At the same time, however, Mystic faced some of the consequences of urban renewal in New London. Displaced downtown residents moved to the areas outside of the city, moving into low-income housing in places such as Fort Hill Homes, which was a noted slum by the 1960s. With the threat of growing low-income neighborhoods closer to Mystic, property owners began to fear both the crime associated with inner cities and a drop in their property values. A historic district would place minimum standards of maintenance upon property owners—which would discourage the rental properties that many associated with neighborhood decline—and preserve the appearance and values of their homes.

In 1976, the Mystic Bridge National Historic District was created on the eastern side of the river, soon followed by a similar district on the western side. Almost immediately, the drawbacks of the historic district became obvious. Improved property values led to higher property taxes, which doubled in the 1970s. While the historic districts preserved both homes and the historic appearance of the town, and prevented the appearance of the gigantic mega-marts that became popular in the 1990s, they also contributed to a near caste system among the people who lived in Mystic.

By the end of the century, middle-class residents could no longer afford these homes, or even afford to live in the area, as property values skyrocketed all along the New England coast. Waterfront property, once the province of the working class, became premium, affordable only to the very rich who had once shunned those districts. In Mystic, high-priced condos appeared on both the east and west sides of the river. The old trolley barn on the west side of the river was also transformed into luxury apartments.

Those who could afford the high property prices and taxes, either as year-round or as summer residents, helped maintain the appearance of Mystic, contributed to its appeal to tourists and sustained its economy as consumers. At the same time, however, the service industry that supported tourism employed the largest number of people as waiters, cooks, dishwashers, hotel staff, fast food and retail clerks, deck hands and even museum educators. The wages for these jobs were low, and most positions were seasonal. Significant portions of the people employed in these positions were college students, but many others were merely working people or immigrants from South America and the former Soviet Union. They crowded into small apartments carved out

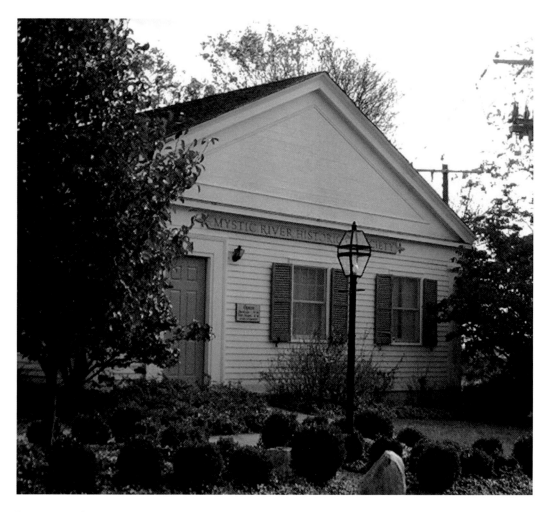

In 1973, the Mystic River Historical Society was founded to preserve local history. The society's collections are housed in a specially designed building, but the building that once served as Portersville Academy is also maintained by the society. *Photo by author, 2006.*

of old houses, or summer cottages during the winter to take advantage of lower rents. Others lived much farther away from Mystic, in towns with less appeal for tourists or developers. Even many professionals working in Mystic's museums, a field with low salaries nationwide, found themselves in the same economically precarious position.

The 1970s were the high point for tourism to historic sites, peaking after decades of growth. By the late 1970s, however, the tourist industry, now the cornerstone of Mystic's economy, began to show signs of change. Rising gas prices and inflation in the mid-1970s affected travel patterns. As early as 1977, the *New London Day* began reporting disappointing receipts for tourism in the area, and the numbers declined steadily in years after. While the decline in historic tourism to the area was long and slow, plans for development modeled on the pre-bicentennial pattern of growth could not succeed. Still, Mystic tourism survived the energy crisis, rising gas prices, inflation and the 1987 stock market crash.

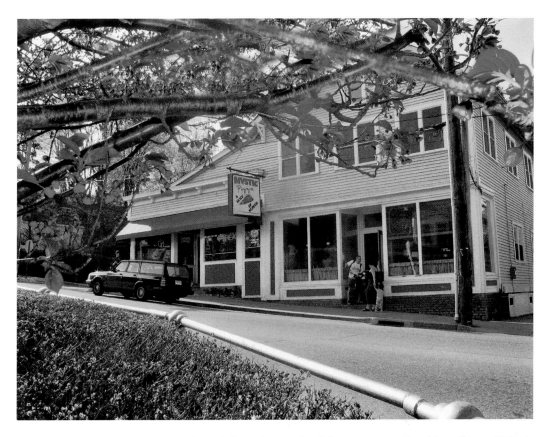

Mystic Pizza served as the namesake for an independent movie of the same name, filmed in and around Mystic in 1987. The restaurant, a popular tourist spot, opened a branch along the route to the Foxwoods Casino and now markets a line of frozen pizzas. *Photo by Stephen Sisk, 2006.*

Hollywood also helped sustain Mystic's economy. In 1987, the small, independent film *Mystic Pizza* opened to critical acclaim. The movie, following the lives of three waitresses in a pizza parlor, was filmed in Mystic and Stonington and starred Lily Taylor, Annabeth Gish and then-unknown Julia Roberts. As the film gained a cult following, bolstered by the successful careers of the three starring actresses in television and independent and feature films, so did Mystic. In 1996, director Steven Spielberg chose Mystic as the backdrop for many of the street scenes in his film *Amistad*, released the following year. Besides being directed by one of the most famous and popular filmmakers in Hollywood, the film also starred Morgan Freeman, Matthew McConaughey and Anthony Hopkins, three actors at high points in their careers, and employed many Mystic residents as extras. *Amistad* was a modest success at both the box office and awards ceremonies, and its popularity led to the creation of Amistad America, Inc. This foundation ordered a replica of the original *Amistad*, and turned to Mystic Seaport's Henry B. duPont Preservation Shipyard for its construction; the ship was launched in 2000.

By the 1990s, however, tourists with less disposable income began to demand more spectacular vacations. Amusement parks that overwhelmed the senses with noise, sights and adrenaline were an example of the type of experience craved on vacations. While amusement parks appealed to a youthful audience, casino resorts offered the same type of experience to adults. Since 1987, Mystic has entered this new era of tourism and, ironically, the Pequot nation has played a major role in the survival of that industry.

In Mystic, the Pequot were last seen as a nation leaving their village on the southwestern banks of the river for a reservation in Ledyard in 1720. Over the centuries, their landholdings had shrunk and their population declined, and reports of the death of the last living Pequot or the last descendant of the Pequot repeatedly appeared in newspapers. By the 1970s, with both genealogical heritage and land claims questioned, only a handful of Pequot survived on the reservation. The national American Indian Movement that sparked a renaissance in Native American culture and political activism had drawn several people with claimed Pequot ancestry to the reservation and galvanized one of the reservation's survivors, Richard "Skip" Hayward. Hayward and Attorney Thomas Tureen began a mission to revive and revitalize the Pequot nation. By 1984, the tribe had gained federal recognition; two years later, the group opened a high-stakes bingo parlor on the reservation as a means of tribal income.

As political entities separate from the U.S. and state governments, Indian tribes within United States borders were free from restrictions on gambling. Facing poverty on the reservation, a desire to maintain the integrity of the tribe itself and no competition from the surrounding Euro-American community, many Native American nations found gambling to be a more than profitable venture. Indeed, many of these tribes operate as businesses in establishing casinos. The Pequot opened their first casino, Foxwoods, in 1992, and it rapidly expanded into a resort. By the end of the decade, Foxwoods included hotels, restaurants, a shopping center, a golf course, a conference center, a concert arena and just about any other diversion to keep tourists occupied for the length of their vacation.

The success of the casino, however, brought many social problems attendant to gambling. Alcoholism, crime, embezzelments, instances of child neglect, drug abuse and especially bankruptcy increased dramatically in the years following the casino's opening, and continued to rise afterward. Traffic to the reservation clogged roads. The resort, able to offer higher wages, the potential for better tips and more consistent employment throughout the year, began to attract service industry workers away from those jobs in the surrounding area. Whereas historic and natural sites had once been the main destination for tourists, they now became side attractions to the casino. Resentment against the Pequot ran high, and the tribal members faced accusations of opportunism.

In Mystic, tensions came to a head in a culture war over a statue. The Pequot were every bit as invested in their own heritage as were the descendants of the European settlers in Mystic, opening a research center in 1998. The center included a museum tracing the history of the Pequot people, as well as a reconstruction of an early Pequot village. The inclusion of a palisade in the exhibit suggests that the village portrays the one that sat on the banks of the Mystic River.

The actual historic location of that village, however, contained a memorial that offended the Pequot. The statue of John Mason had been erected in 1889 with every intention of glorifying the massacre of the Pequot on that site. Sensibilities had changed during the intervening century, as had the understanding of the multicultural history

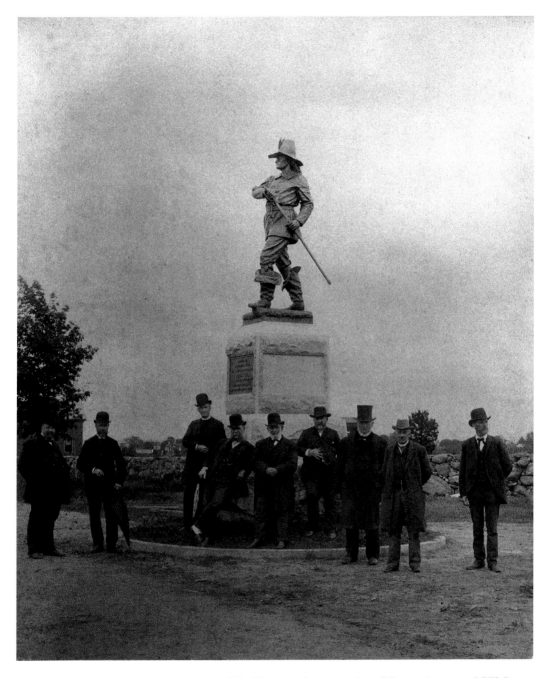

In 1889, citizens of Mystic erected a statue to John Mason at the intersection of Pequot Avenue and Clift Street, near the original location of the Pequot village that he had attacked in 1637. The attack was referred to as a "heroic deed" on a plaque at the base of the monument. *Mystic Seaport Collection, Mystic, Connecticut, #1961.1221.*

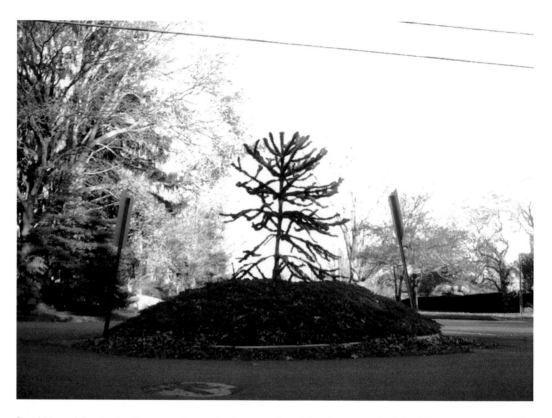

In 1992, activists in the Pequot nation and others petitioned for the removal of the Mason monument. The John Mason Statue Advisory Committee was formed, and after much debate voted to remove the statue to Wethersfield, where Mason had once lived. No markers of the 1637 events remain. *Photo by author, 2006.*

of the United States. In 1992, the Pequot demanded the removal and destruction of the statue that celebrated the perpetrator of an act of genocide against their own ancestors. The Mystic citizens protested, seeing the statue as commemorating an event that led to the settlement of Mystic by their own ancestors and as a memorial to the citizens who had erected the statue in the previous century.

Emotions ran high, and Groton town meetings on the subject became intense and heated. A commission was appointed to research the merits of the arguments on both sides, and to recommend a solution. In 1996, both parties reached a compromise. The town would remove the statue and send it to Wethersfield, where Mason had lived, rather than destroy it. No other memorial appeared to note the events that occurred on that site. Meanwhile, in 1992, the Pequot set a small monument on Fort Hill, on the site of Eva Butler's Indian Museum.

This volume ends as it began, in a confrontation between Native Americans and Europeans. The Pequot had once dominated the region surrounding the Mystic River, and three hundred years later, their descendants reemerged as a major force in the economy of the same area. Despite the literary symmetry of this latest conflict, it is really only the most recent phase of Mystic's history.

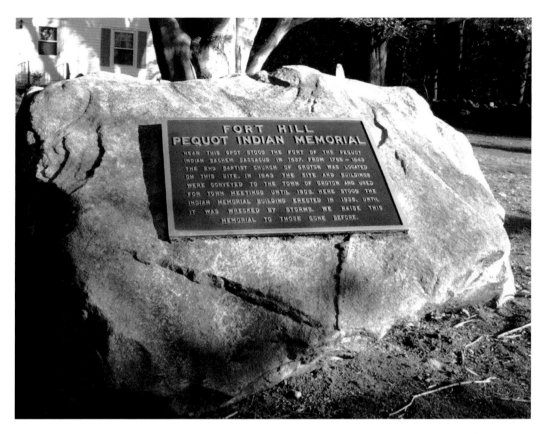

This plaque, erected by Boy Scouts, commemorates the seventeenth-century Pequot village that stood on this site at Fort Hill. Earlier, in the 1930s, Eva L. Butler had founded a small museum dedicated to the Native Americans of the region. The museum fell into disrepair, and was finally destroyed in 1979. *Photo by author, 2006.*

This volume ends, too, just before the terrorist attacks on the Pentagon and the World Trade Center on September 11, 2001. That disaster, and the wars on Afghanistan and Iraq, caused a decrease in air travel as Americans became either afraid of flying or annoyed by the increased security measures at airports. Long-distance car trips also became less feasible in the face of skyrocketing gas prices. All of these factors have impacted the tourism, be it to historic sites or casinos, on which Mystic's economy has been based for over half a century. Whether these latest events have effectively altered Mystic's development remains a question to be answered by historians of the future.

RESEARCHING MYSTIC

This volume provides a survey history of Mystic, Connecticut, in which the broad narrative of events has taken precedent over many smaller, isolated stories. In the interest of space, time and the nature of the form, many interesting stories have not received full treatment. This bibliography should guide interested readers toward sources that will allow them to pursue a particular subject for more detail. This bibliography is neither comprehensive nor exhaustive, representing only the most important works on Mystic.

Editorial Consultation
William Peterson
Director, Mystic Seaport, The Museum of America & the Sea

ARCHIVES

Connecticut Historical Society, Hartford, CT
Connecticut State Library, Hartford, CT
Groton Public Library, Groton, CT
Indian and Colonial Research Center, Old Mystic, CT
Mashantucket Pequot Museum and Research Center, Mashantucket, CT
Mystic River Historical Society, Mystic, CT
Mystic Seaport Museum, Collections Research Center, Mystic, CT
New London Historical Society, New London, CT
Stonington Historical Society, Stonington, CT

SELECTED BIBLIOGRAPHY

Allyn, James. *Major John Mason's Great Island.* Mystic, CT: Ray N. Bohlander, 1976.

Anderson, Virginia B. *Maritime Mystic.* Mystic, CT: Marine Historical Association, 1962.

Baughman, James P. *The Mallorys of Mystic: Six Generations of American Maritime Enterprise.* Middletown, CT: Wesleyan University Press, 1972.

Buel, Richard, Jr., and J. Bard McNulty, eds. *Connecticut Observed: Three Centuries of Visitors' Impressions, 1676–1940.* Hartford, CT: Acorn Club, 1999.

Burrows, Roscoe K. *Village Fire Fighters, 1883–1942: A History of the Mystic Hook and Ladder Co., No. 1, of Mystic, Connecticut.* Stonington, CT: Stonington Publishing, 1942.

Caulkins, Frances Manwaring. *History of New London, Connecticut, from the First Survey of the Coast in 1612 to 1852.* Hartford, CT: Case, Tiffany, and Co., 1852.

Cave, Alfred A. *The Pequot War.* Amherst: University of Massachusetts Press, 1996.

Clarke, Helen May. *An Account of My Life: The Childhood Journals of Helen May Clarke, 1915–1926.* Mystic, CT: Mystic River Historical Society, 1997.

Comrie, Marilyn, and Carol W. Kimball. *Union Baptist Church of Mystic, Connecticut.* Mystic, CT: Union Baptist Church, 1987.

Cutler, Carl C. *Mystic: The Story of a Small New England Seaport.* Mystic, CT: Marine Historical Association, 1945.

SELECTED BIBLIOGRAPHY

Decker, Robert Owen. *The Whaling City: A History of New London.* Chester, CT: Pequot Press, 1976.

DeForest, John W. *History of the Indians of Connecticut from the Earliest Known Period to 1850.* Hartford, CT: William James Hamesley, 1852.

Eisler, Kim Isaac. *Revenge of the Pequots: How a Small Native American Tribe Created the World's Most Profitable Casino.* New York: Simon and Schuster, 2001.

Eldredge, Charles Q. *The Story of a Connecticut Life.* Troy, NY: Allen Books and Printing Company, 1919.

Frost, John. *Indian Wars of the United States, from the Discovery to the Present Time, With Accounts of the Origin, Manners, Superstitions, etc. of the Aborigines.* Philadelphia: Leary and Getz, 1853.

Goodman, Mary Virginia. *Noank Notes: Newspaper Columns of Mary Virginia Goodman.* Edited by Carol W. Kimball. Groton, CT: Groton Public Library and Information Center, 1990.

Gouldsmith Speck, Frank, and John Dyneley Prince. *Glossary of the Mohegan-Pequot Language.* Lancaster, PA: New Era Printing Co., 1904.

Greenhalgh, Kathleen. *A History of Old Mystic, 1600–1909.* Privately printed, 1999.

———. *A History of West Mystic, 1600–1985.* Groton, CT: Groton Public Library and Information Center, 1986.

Hauptman, Laurence M., and James D. Wherry. *The Pequots in Southern New England: The Rise and Fall of an American Indian Nation.* Norman: University of Oklahoma Press, 1990.

Haynes, William. *Captain John Gallup: Master Mariner and Indian Trader.* Stonington, CT: Pequot Press, 1964.

———. *Stonington Chronology, 1694–1976: Being a Year-by-year Record of the American Way of Life in a Connecticut Town.* Chester, CT: Pequot Press, 1949.

Hempstead, Joshua. *Diary of Joshua Hempstead of New London, Connecticut, Covering a Period of Forty-Seven Years, from September, 1711 to November, 1758.* New London, CT: New London County Historical Society, 1901.

Jensen, Barbara Neff. *Mystic Families and More Memories of a Native.* Groton, CT: Groton Public Library and Information Center, 1990.

Kimball, Carol W. *The Groton Story*. Groton, CT: Groton Public Library and Information Center, 1991.

———. *Historic Glimpses: Recollections of Days Past in the Mystic River Valley*. Mystic, CT: Flat Hammock Press, 2005.

———. *The Poquonnock Bridge Story*. Groton, CT: Groton Public Library, 1984.

Knight, Sarah Kemble. *The Journal of Madame Knight*. Edited by Malcolm Freiberg. Boston: Massachusetts Historical Society, 1971.

Marshall, Benjamin Tinkam. *A Modern History of New London County*. 2 vols. New York: Lewis Historical Publishing Co., 1922.

Miner, Thomas. *The Diary of Thomas Miner, Stonington, Connecticut, 1653–1684*. Edited by Sidney Miner and George D. Stanton. New London, CT: Day Publishing Co., 1899.

Noble, William F., and Kristen Noble. *The Archaeology of Connecticut*. Storrs, CT: Bibliogpola Press, 1999.

Orr, Charles, ed. *History of the Pequot War: The Contemporary Accounts of Mason, Underhill, Vincent, and Gardener*. Cleveland: Helman-Taylor Company, 1897.

Peterson, William N. *"Mystic Built": Ships and Shipyards of the Mystic River, Connecticut, 1784–1919*. Mystic, CT: Mystic Seaport Museum, 1989.

Peterson, William N., and Peter M. Coop. *Historic Buildings at Mystic Seaport Museum*. Mystic, CT: Mystic Seaport Museum, Inc., 1985.

Radune, Richard A. *Pequot Plantation: The Story of an Early Colonial Settlement*. Branford, CT: Research in Time Publications, 2005.

Read, Eleanor B. *Mystic Memories*. Privately printed, 1980.

Trumbull, Benjamin. *A Compendium of the Indian Wars in New England*. Hartford, CT: Edward Valentine Mitchell, 1926.

Wheeler, Grace. *Grace Wheeler's Memories*. Chester, CT: Pequot Press, 1948. First published 1907.

———. *The Homes of Our Ancestors in Stonington, Connecticut*. Salem, MA: Newcomb and Gauss, 1903.

INDEX

A

Ackley, Carl 130
African Americans 42, 46
alcohol and liquor 33, 91, 97, 104
Alien Property Custodian Commission 84
Allen Spool & Printing Company 82, 84
Amistad 135
Amistad America, Inc. 135
antislavery movement 69
Armistice Day 110
Arnold, Benedict 54
artisans and craftsmen 43, 47, 59, 65, 66, 79
artists 87, 94, 95, 98, 121, 130
Ashby, George W. 67
Association of Pawcatuck People 38, 39
Avery, James 40
Avery, Stephen 46
Avery Point 90, 129

B

baby boom 127, 129
banks and banking 67
Barber, John 58
baseball 99, 100, 102
Batty, John 65
Batty, Oliver 65
Batty, William 65
Beebe & King 66
Beebe family 35, 41
Bell, Alexander Graham 116
bicentennial 132, 133, 134
bicycling 100, 102
blacksmiths and shipsmiths 43, 65
Blinman, Robert 35
Block, Adrien 13
Block Island, Rhode Island 14, 22, 56
Bogue Town 94, 107
Boston 15, 48, 49, 52, 59, 65, 69, 92
Bridgeport, Connecticut 131
Broadway School 95, 113
Broughton Company 81
Bryan, William Jennings 105
buildings and homes
  Buckingham Hall house 131
  Central Hall 102, 103
  Denison homestead 126
  Froshinn Hall 108
  Greenman brothers homes 66, 74
  Mystic National Bank 126
  Silas E. Burrows home 60, 116
  Strand Theater 103
  Whitehall Manor 131

Burrows, Enoch 56
Burrows, Robert 41, 46
Burrows, Silas 91
Burrows, Silas E. 57, 59, 60, 63
Bushy Point 90, 100
businesses 43, 47, 59, 61, 63, 64, 65, 66, 69, 73, 78, 79, 81, 82, 85, 86
Butler, Eva L. 111, 126, 130, 138

C

C.A. Fenner & Company 82
camps and camping 92, 93, 95, 98, 130
Cape Horn 62, 63
capitalists 59, 60, 62, 79
cars 11, 84, 122, 131, 132, 134, 136, 139
casinos 95, 97, 98, 121, 136, 139
Cassacinamon, Robin 36
centennial celebrations 109
Chamber of Commerce 105
Charles Beebe & Son 65
Charles Q. Eldredge Museum 121, 124
Charles W. Morgan 121, 126, 131
Cheney Globe Company 82
Chesebrough, William 33
children 13, 26, 30, 35, 42
China trade 60
Chipman, Thomas 46
churches 37, 38, 41, 42, 50, 66, 70, 107
  Union Baptist Church 73, 85, 110, 122
Civil War regiments, Mystic 70
Civil War Soldiers' and Sailors' Monument 110
Clarke, Helen May 91, 94, 97, 98, 107
Clift, Amos, II 66
Clift, Ira H. 67
Clift, Isaac D. 66, 67
Clift, Nathaniel 57, 90
Clift, William 67
Climax Tube Company 84
coastal trade 38, 51, 60, 70, 71, 74
Coates, Julia Beebe 95
Cold War 86, 127, 129
Committees of Correspondence 52
company towns 59, 66
Coneau, Benjamin 98

Confederate States of America 74
Connecticut 11, 13, 14, 18, 19, 22, 23, 24, 30, 33, 34, 35, 37, 38, 39, 40, 46, 54, 70, 78, 85, 94, 111, 117, 121
Connecticut Cabinet Company 85, 86
Connecticut General Court 30, 31, 33, 34, 35, 36, 37, 38, 39
Connecticut River 14, 15, 18, 19, 22, 24, 34, 40, 43
Cooper Laboratories 86
cotton trade 60, 63, 74
Cottrell, Gallup & Company 66, 81
Cottrell, Joseph 66, 67, 71, 81
Coxey's Army 105
Crompton-Knowles 86
Crowther, H.A. 79
Cuba 71, 75
Culver, Edward 43
Culver, Samuel 42, 43

D

Dahlia and Pedestrian Club 109
Daughters of the American Revolution, Fanny Ledyard Chapter 109
David Crockett 63
David D. Mallory & Company 67
Davis, Charles H. 94
Davis-Standard Company 86
Dean, James 79
Dean, James, Jr. 47
deforestation 47, 85
Delameter, Cornelius 75
Delameter Ironworks 75
Denison, Ebenezer 57
Denison, Frederick 57
Denison, George 35, 38, 39, 41
Denison, Isaac, Jr. 57
Denison, Isaac W. 60, 67
Denison, Walter 100
Denison family 41
Denison Society 111, 126
disease and sickness 15, 39, 51
Doyle, Louis 84
Dudley, Lyman 65, 66
Durham Enders Company 85, 86

E

E.S. Belden & Son 82
E. & L. Watrous 82
economy and economic developments 11,
    41, 45, 46, 47, 56, 59, 63, 70, 71, 77,
    78, 79, 81, 82, 84, 85, 86
Eldredge, Charles, Jr. 52
Eldredge, Charles Q. 87, 124
Electric Boat Company 85
Elm Grove Cemetery 110, 131
embargo acts 56
Endicott, John 22, 23
Enforcement Acts 52
England 15, 22, 24, 33, 39, 45, 51
English government 15, 45, 47, 49, 51, 52
English navy 51, 52, 53, 54, 56
entertainment 90, 93, 95, 99, 100, 102,
    103, 104, 105, 108, 119, 136
entrepreneurs 46, 59, 75, 78, 82
Eureka rolling chairs 82

F

farming 31, 33, 36, 37, 38, 40, 41, 43, 44,
    45, 46, 47, 49, 50, 52, 58, 65, 69, 78,
    81, 104, 105, 130
Federal Highway Act, 1921 122
Federal Highway Act, 1955 131
ferries 41, 44, 48, 50, 61
fire departments 116, 117
Fish, James 42
Fish, John 42
Fish, Nathan G. 67
Fish, Simeon 67
fishing 45, 50, 51, 53, 56, 57, 62, 64, 77,
    81, 104, 108
Fish family 91
Florida 56, 60
Flying Cloud 63
Fort Griswold 53, 54
Fort Hill 13, 36, 50, 62, 138
Fort Hill Homes 86, 129, 133
Fort Hill Indian Memorial Association
    111, 126
Fort Hill memorial 138
Fort Rachel 57, 97

Fort Trumbull 53, 54
France 15, 51, 52, 56
Franklin, Benjamin 49
Freeman, Morgan 135

G

G.S. Allyn & Company 81
G.W. Packer & Co. 81
Galena 70, 73
Gallup, John 22, 41, 43
Gallup, John, Jr. 35, 40
Gallup, Samuel 47
Gallup, William 43, 47
Gallup family 52
Galveston, Texas 75
gambling 95, 136
Gardiner, Henry 100
Gardiner, Lion 22, 23
Gaskill, Ben 102
Gates, Ann Borodell Denison 126
Gilbert Morgan & Company 66
Gilbert Morgan Company 81
Goodman, Mary Virginia 119, 127
Good Hope, Connecticut 18, 19
governors 31, 35, 39
Grant, William N. 66
Great Depression 78, 84, 94, 98, 121, 127,
    129
Greenfield, Michigan 131
Greenman, Clark 60
Greenman, George 60
Greenman, Silas, Jr. 60
Greenman, Silas, Sr. 60
Greenman, Thomas 60, 104
Greenman brothers 66, 67, 70, 75, 79
Greenman Manufacturing Company 63,
    66, 79
Grinnell, Amos 60, 73
Grinnell, Charles 79
Griswold, Florence 94
Groton, Connecticut 44, 46, 47, 48, 49,
    50, 52, 54, 60, 61, 82, 86, 87, 90,
    100, 105, 123, 129, 131, 138
    Avery Point 77
    Burnett's Corners 81, 82, 95, 113

INDEX

Groton Bank 48, 53, 59, 61, 62
Groton Long Point 11, 47, 52, 57, 131
Gungywump 13
Poquonnoc 21, 41, 50, 62, 82, 86, 100, 113, 126, 129
Groton submarine base 85, 86

H

Haley, Frederick 57
Haley, Jeremiah 56, 57
Haley, Simeon 57
Hamilton, Alexander 48
Hardy, Thomas 57
Hartford 18, 19, 22, 24, 30, 31, 38, 46, 78
Hasbrouck Motor Company 81
Hayne, John 35
Hayward, Richard "Skip" 136
Hedge, John (or William) 26
Hill, Mason Crary 73, 77
history 121, 124, 126, 127, 130, 131, 133, 136
Hollywood 135
Holmes, Isaac D. 66
Holmes, Jeremiah 56, 57
Hopkins, Anthony 135
Hopkinton, Rhode Island 49
Howe, Julia Ward 91
Hoxie, Benjamin F. 67, 90, 117
hurricane, 1675 40
hurricane, 1938 85, 109
Hyde, James 79
Hyde, John 46, 47, 63

I

immigrants and immigration 39, 65, 90, 104, 107, 108, 113, 133
imperialism 90
Indian and Colonial Research Center 111, 126, 127
Indian trade 13, 15, 18, 19, 20, 24, 31, 33, 40
Industrial Revolution 58, 66, 78, 86, 92, 104, 105
industries 47, 62, 63, 66, 69, 73, 77, 78, 79, 81, 82, 85, 86

Interstate Highway Act, 1956 131
investing and investments 53, 59, 60, 63, 64, 66, 71, 75, 79, 82
Irons, Dexter 60, 73
Iroquois Five Nations 14, 15, 18, 19, 22, 30

J

J&W Batty 65
J.W. Lathrop & Company 81
J. & W.P. Randall 66
James Campbell & John N. Colby 65
Jobe, Mary L. 92, 93, 130
Johl, William 85
Johnson, Charles 81
Johnson & Denison 65, 81
John Mason statue 136

K

Ketcham, Fred 105
Kimball, Carol W. 126, 127
Kingston, Rhode Island 40
Knight, Sarah Kemble 47, 48

L

labor and laborers 45, 46, 47, 59, 60, 61, 64, 66, 73, 84, 85, 94, 104, 105, 108, 119, 122, 123, 133, 136
Lake, Margaret 35
Lamb, John 43, 46, 47
Lantern Hill 49, 82
Latham, Cary 41
Lathrop, James 81
Lathrop & Northrup 66, 81
Lathrop Engine Company 82, 86
Ledyard, Connecticut 90, 136
Ledyard, William 54
Lee, Daniel 51
Leeds family 59
Liberty Pole 52, 70, 109
livestock 35, 36, 38, 41, 43, 45, 46, 52
lodging
  boardinghouses 66
  Hoxie House 90, 118
  Mystic Island hotel 90, 95

taverns 43, 50, 90
tenements 105, 107
U.S. Hotel 90
Long Island 14, 27, 53, 85
Long Island Sound 21, 44, 52, 56, 97
Loomis, John 51
Ludlow, Roger 20
lumber 43, 47, 60, 66, 73, 75, 81
Lyme, Connecticut 94
Lyme Art Association 94
Lyme Art Gallery 94

M

machinery 66, 78, 79, 81
Maine 15, 18, 75
Mallory, Charles 59, 60, 62, 63, 66, 67, 71, 73, 75, 77
Mallory, Charles H. 67, 75, 77, 79, 109, 111, 113
Mallory, David 60, 67, 71, 79, 81, 82
Mallory family 60
Manhattan 18, 52
manufacturing 11, 41, 43, 45, 46, 47, 49, 50, 52, 58, 59, 63, 71, 73, 77, 78, 79, 81, 82, 84, 86, 87, 105, 120, 121, 123
Marine Historical Association 111, 121, 124, 126, 130, 131
Markham Rock Quarry 82
Mason, John 24, 26, 27, 30, 33, 35, 36, 39, 40
Mason, John, Jr. 40
Masons Island 35, 50, 57, 81, 82, 85, 93, 95, 98
Masons Island Yacht Club 85, 98
Mason family 41
Massachusetts 19, 33, 35, 37, 39, 40, 41, 42, 79
Massachusetts Bay 15, 18, 19, 20, 22, 23, 24, 31, 33, 34, 35, 37, 38, 39
Massasoit 40
Maxson, William E. 67
McConaughey, Matthew 135
McKinley, William 105
merchants 51, 52, 56, 60, 73, 123, 129

Metacom, "King Philip" 40
Miantonomo 24, 33
middle class 104, 133
militia and volunteers 24, 33, 34, 39, 40, 46, 51, 52, 54, 57, 58, 70
veterans 33, 39, 41
mills 31, 43, 46, 47, 63, 66, 70, 75, 78, 79, 84
cotton 47
fulling 43, 47, 78, 79
grist 43, 46, 47, 78
saw 43, 47, 78
wind 46
Miner, Hempsted 46
Miner, Thomas 35, 37, 38, 40, 41
Mixtuxet Brook 47
Mohegan 20, 33, 35
Montaines 81
Montgomery, William 54
Morgan, James 36
Mott, Lucretia 91
movies, motion pictures and films 95, 103, 135
museums 124, 126, 130, 131, 132, 134
Mystic
Adams Point 60, 121
Baptist Hill 122
Greenmanville 63, 66, 79, 107, 110
Head of the River (Old Mystic) 42, 43, 44, 46, 47, 49, 50, 56, 61, 63, 66, 67, 75, 79, 87
Lower Mystic 44, 46, 61
Mystic Bridge (village) 61, 66, 75, 87, 116
Mystic River (village) 62, 70, 74, 87, 113
naming 11, 87, 90
Old Mystic 85, 87, 116, 119, 126, 131
Pistol Point 46, 47, 50, 56
Porter's Rocks 26, 82
Portersville 44, 50, 52, 56, 61, 62, 116
Willow Point 90
Mystic-Noank library 113
Mystic Academy 113
Mystic Aquarium 11, 132
Mystic Art Association 95

INDEX

Mystic Bicycle Club 102
Mystic Club 102, 113
Mystic Community Club 103
Mystic Cornet Band 74, 103
Mystic Distilling Company 82
Mystic Garden Club 109, 130
Mystic Grange 105
Mystic Industrial Corporation 79
Mystic Iron Works 71, 79, 81
Mystic Island 51, 90, 95, 130
Mystic Lyceum 103
Mystic Manufacturing Company 47, 58,
    63, 79, 85, 126
Mystic Men's Club 87
Mystic Merchants' Association 129
Mystic Oral School 113
Mystic Pizza 135
Mystic Power Company 118
Mystic River 11, 15, 30, 31, 33, 35, 37, 38,
    39, 41, 42, 43, 44, 45, 46, 47, 48, 49,
    50, 51, 52, 54, 56, 57, 60, 62, 63, 65,
    66, 69, 77, 79, 82, 87, 90, 94, 97, 98,
    104, 119, 121, 136
    Siccanemos 13, 21
Mystic River drawbridge 61, 62, 63, 75,
    84, 90, 94, 102, 103, 105, 107, 109,
    119, 121, 122
Mystic River Hardware Manufacturing
    Company 81
Mystic River Valley 35, 40, 45, 59, 78
Mystic Rod and Gun Club 99
Mystic Seaport 11, 60, 135
Mystic Water Company 117
Mystic Wheel Club 102
Mystic Woolen Company 79, 81

N

Narragansett 14, 15, 18, 19, 20, 22, 23, 24,
    26, 30, 31, 33, 35, 39, 40
Narragansett Bay 15, 18, 33, 39, 43, 52
Native Americans 13, 15, 18, 19, 22, 24,
    26, 30, 33, 34, 36, 37, 38, 39, 40, 42,
    43, 44, 90, 126, 136, 138
Nauyaug Yacht Club 93, 98
Netherlands 13, 14, 15, 18, 19, 20, 22, 33

Newport, Rhode Island 44, 52, 56, 92
New Bedford, Massachusetts 63, 126
New England 19, 20, 38, 39, 40, 41, 42,
    45, 48, 49, 52, 63, 70, 78, 85, 95,
    123, 130, 131, 133
New Haven, Connecticut 48, 131
New London, Connecticut 35, 40, 41, 43,
    44, 48, 51, 52, 53, 54, 56, 59, 63, 95,
    100, 119, 123, 129, 133
New Orleans 75
New York 44, 48, 52, 56, 60, 65, 69, 75,
    77, 82, 92, 94
New York state 13, 71, 75
Niantics 20
Niantic River 13, 20
Noank, Connecticut 50, 56, 95, 113, 119,
    127, 131
Norwich, Connecticut 49, 50, 52, 63, 82,
    86
Noyes, George W. 67
Noyes, Henry B. 67
Noyes, Joseph 105

O

Oceanic Woolen Company 79, 81
Oldham, John 22, 24, 34, 35
Old Sturbridge Village 131
Openhym, William 84
Outdoor Art Festival 130

P

Packer, Daniel 56, 82
Packer, Eldredge 56
Packer, Joseph 52
Packer, Tony 105
Packer's Tar Soap 82, 85, 86
Packer family 41, 50, 59
Palmer, Walter 38
Palmer family 53
Park, Robert 35
Parke, Thomas 35
Parke family 41
parks and preserves 91, 130
Pawcatuck 13
Pawcatuck, Connecticut 24, 38, 39, 97

Pawcatuck River 13, 20, 24, 31, 33, 37, 38, 39, 40, 41, 43, 118
Pawtucket, Rhode Island 131
peace meeting 90, 91, 92, 95
Pequot 11, 13, 14, 15, 18, 19, 20, 22, 23, 24, 26, 27, 30, 31, 33, 34, 35, 36, 38, 39, 40, 43, 46, 121, 136, 138
Empire 14, 15, 18, 19, 20, 24, 27, 30, 33, 34
Foxwoods Casino 11, 136
genocide 24, 30
Mashantucket Pequot Museum and Research Center 136
Mashantucket Pequot reservation 11, 36, 136
Mystic fort 13, 24, 26, 136
Pequot Lodge of the Modern Woodmen of America 99
Pequot Plantation (New London) 33, 35, 38, 40
Peru 75
petitions 38, 69
Pfizer 129
photographers and photography 95
piracy and privateering 51, 52, 53, 54, 56, 97
Plymouth 15, 18, 33, 35, 40
political parties 69, 73, 105
population growth 39, 65, 73, 86
Poquonnoc Driving Park 100, 129
ports 51, 52
press gangs and impressment 52, 56, 57
Price, Garrett 95
prisoners 22, 26
Progressive era 104, 105, 113
Prohibition 97
Providence 44, 48, 49, 50, 90, 132

Q

Quiambaug Cove 35

R

Radicioni, Joseph 98
railroad 69, 82, 85, 90, 107, 108
Ram's Island 51, 90

Randall, Jedediah 66, 67, 70
Reliance Machine Company 66, 71, 79, 81
Rhode Island 39, 45, 46, 79
Richmond, David O. 77
rivers and waterways 13, 41, 49, 50
roads and highways 38, 41, 44, 45, 48, 49, 50, 51, 61
Allyn Street 131, 132
Bank Square 62, 85
Boston Post Road 44, 46, 48, 49, 50
Clift Street 110
construction 47, 48, 49, 50, 87, 122, 123
Exit 89 (I-95) 131
Exit 90 (I-95) 131, 132
Greenmanville Avenue 84, 108, 131
Holmes Street 84, 90, 102, 117
Main Street 84, 105, 110, 113, 122
Main Street, East 90, 103, 117
Main Street, West 62, 73, 85
New London Road 50, 84, 122
Old Pequot Trail 31, 41, 43, 48, 49, 50
Pequot Avenue 110
River Road 50, 124
U.S. Interstate 95 (I-95) 41, 121, 131
U.S. Route 1 84, 86, 122, 123, 126, 129, 130, 131
Water Street 62, 94, 107, 119, 122
Willow Street 44, 49, 61, 66
Road Society 111
Roberts, Julia 135
Rossie, Ernest 79
Rossie, John 79
Rossie, Thomas 79
Rossie family 84, 108
Rossie Velvet Mill 79, 84, 86, 107
Rotten Row 107
rumrunning 97
Russell Welles Company 82

S

sailmaking 59, 60, 66
sail loft 59, 66, 75
saloons 97, 105
saltworks 47
salvage business 60

INDEX

Santin, Aldo 84

Santin, Joe 84

Santin, Sebastian 84

Santin and Sons 84

Sassacus 14, 20, 21, 25, 30, 126

Saybrook, Connecticut 22, 23, 24, 27, 82, 131

Scholfield, Everett A. 95

September 11, 2001 11, 139

servants 45

service industry 133, 136

settlers, English 15, 18, 19, 20, 22, 23, 24, 26, 31, 33, 35, 36, 39, 40, 43, 45, 51, 52, 53, 126

settlers, European 13, 14, 15, 20, 30, 43, 136, 138

shipbuilding 11, 45, 47, 52, 56, 58, 59, 60, 61, 63, 64, 65, 66, 67, 69, 71, 73, 74, 77, 78, 79, 81, 82, 87, 105, 120, 123

shipping 46, 51, 60, 63, 69

shipyards 56, 59, 60, 61, 63, 64, 65, 66, 71, 73, 75, 77, 79, 81, 104, 129

  Benjamin Morrill 56

  C.H. Mallory & Co. 75

  Charles Mallory & Sons 65, 66, 79

  Eastern Shipbuilding Company 77, 82

  Electric Boat Company 77

  George Greenman & Co. 60, 65, 66, 131

  Gilbert Transportation Company 75

  Henry B. duPont Preservation 135

  Hill & Grinnell 73, 75, 77

  Irons & Grinnell 73

  Leeds 56, 59

  M.B. MacDonald & Sons 75

  Maxson, Fish & Company 60, 67

  Maxson & Fish 73

  New York Ship & Engine Company 77, 82

  Pendleton Brothers 75

  Post 77, 82, 84, 97, 98

  West Mystic Boat Company 97

shops and shopping 66, 67, 82, 86, 87, 105, 121, 129, 131, 133, 136

Shore Line Bowling League 103

silex 82

Sirtex Printing Company 85, 86

Slaughterhouse Hill 50

slaves and slavery 19, 30, 42, 45, 46, 63, 69

Smith, Venture 46

Society of Mystic Artists 95

Soderberg, Yngve 95

Sosos 20

Southern New England Telephone Company 118

South America 60

souvenirs 99

Spanish gunboat incident 75

Spicer, Abel 52

Spicer, Elihu 113

Spielberg, Steven 135

stagecoaches 49, 50

Standard Machine Company 82, 85, 86

Stanton, Thomas 22, 24, 30, 33, 38, 39, 46

Stillman, Charles K. 126

Stone, John 19, 20, 22, 24, 34

Stonington, Connecticut 33, 39, 40, 41, 42, 44, 46, 47, 49, 52, 57, 61, 82, 87, 97, 100, 108, 119, 126, 131, 135

  Southington 39

  Stonington Borough 53, 56, 57, 108, 123

  Wequetequock 33

Stonington Historical Society 111, 124, 131

Stonington Temperance Union 104

Stoughton, Thomas 34

summer residents 93, 95, 98, 120, 131, 132, 133

Sunoco Corporation 84, 86

Swansea, Rhode Island 40

T

Tatobem 19, 20

taxes and taxation 52, 79

Taylor, Lily 135

Taylor Woolen Mill 79

telegraph 87, 90, 118

telephones 87, 118

Tenement Building Association 105

textiles 43, 46, 47, 53, 62, 63, 70, 78, 79, 81

Thames River 11, 13, 21, 27, 30, 31, 33, 35, 37, 38, 41, 43, 48, 49, 50, 53, 54, 56, 59, 63, 77, 82, 85, 86, 118, 129
  Pequot River 21, 23, 24
Thompson, William 38
Tingley, George 95
tourists and tourism 11, 77, 82, 86, 87, 90, 91, 92, 93, 94, 98, 99, 105, 111, 119, 120, 121, 123, 124, 127, 129, 130, 131, 132, 133, 134, 135, 136, 139
Treaty of Hartford 30, 33, 38
trolleys 84, 87, 118, 119, 133
Turner, Philip 51
Turner, William 22

U

U.S. Coast Guard 77, 82, 121, 129
U.S. government 56, 69, 75, 79
U.S. Navy 77
U.S. Postal Service 49, 50
U.S. Signal Corp 85
Uncas 20, 24, 26, 27, 30, 33
Underhill, John 22, 24, 26, 34
United Colonies of New England 35, 38, 39, 40
Universal Peace Union 90, 91, 92
urban renewal 133

V

Village Improvement League 108

W

Waite, Elmer 95
Wampanoag 40
Wamsutta 40
wars 11
  American Revolution 44, 47, 52, 53, 54, 56, 78, 109
  Anglo-Dutch Wars 33
  Battle of Antietam 70
  Battle of Drury's Bluff 70
  Battle of Gettysburg 70
  Battle of Port Hudson 70
  Battle of Stonington 57
  Civil War 64, 67, 69, 77, 81, 90, 95, 99, 103, 110
  English Civil War 35
  Great Swamp Battle (King Philip's War) 40
  imperial wars 51
  King Philip's War 41
  Pequot War 23, 24, 30, 31, 33, 34, 35, 38, 39, 41, 43, 110, 126
  Seven Years' War 52
  Spanish-American War 91
  War of 1812 44, 47, 56, 59, 78
  World War I 77, 81, 82, 84, 90, 93, 94, 95, 97, 98, 110, 119, 121, 122, 131
  World War II 78, 85, 99, 121, 126, 127, 130
Watch Hill, Rhode Island 90
Weck Corporation 86
Wequash 20
Westerly, Rhode Island 48, 49, 60
West Indies trade 19, 38, 51, 56
West Mystic Motor Company 81
Wethersfield, Connecticut 19, 22, 23, 138
whalers and whaling 53, 56, 60, 63, 64, 71, 74
Wheeler, Grace Denison 126
White, G.W. Blunt 84, 98
Wilcox, Stephen 47
Williams, Charles P. 100
Windsor, Connecticut 19, 24
Winthrop, John, Jr. 31, 35, 39, 43, 46, 100
Winthrop, John, Sr. 35
women 13, 23, 26, 30, 35, 47, 91, 92, 104, 109, 126, 127
Woodbridge, Dudley 50, 52
World War I memorial 110

Y

yachts and yachting 77, 81, 84, 98
Yankee Homecoming 131

ABOUT THE AUTHOR

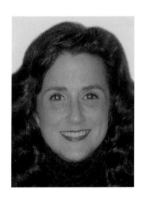

Leigh Fought first came to Mystic, Connecticut, as a summer intern at Mystic Seaport in 2001. Other obligations took her to Indianapolis, where she served as associate editor of the Frederick Douglass Papers, and to Boston, where she earned a master's degree in library science. She returned to Mystic in 2005, working as a manuscripts assistant in the G.W. Blunt White Library of Mystic Seaport. Fought holds a PhD in U.S. history from the University of Houston and is the author of *Southern Womanhood and Slavery: A Biography of Louisa S. McCord, 1810–1870.*

Visit us at
www.historypress.net